Reframing and Rethinking Collaboration in Higher Education and Beyond

Reframing and Rethinking Collaboration in Higher Education and Beyond delves deep into a Taxonomy of Collaboration underpinned by mindful choices – being present, aware, non-judgemental, curious and open – while also considering your and others' strengths.

In looking at how higher degree research students and early career researchers can approach collaboration, this book unpacks what collaboration is and points to the specific knowledge, skills, and abilities associated with achieving collaborative advantage. Covering a range of issues in a variety of contexts, this book:

- Helps you understand the meaning and value of working collaboratively.
- Prepares you for success in collaborative academic and postgraduate career activities.
- Invites you to use models, including the Taxonomy of Collaboration, to plan your collaborative projects.
- Explains options for different situations through realistic examples of commonly experienced collaborative issues or problems.

- Encourages you to think about collaboration from a strengths-based approach.
- Offers practical strategies you can use to plan, organise and participate in collaborative activities, including ways to deal with problems and resolve conflicts.

Full of practical tips, case studies, real life situations and lived experiences, this book offers strategies that can be used in online or hybrid collaborations and is ideal reading for anyone interested in finding out how to make collaborative practice work for them.

Narelle Lemon is an associate professor in Education located in the Department of Education, Faculty of Health, Arts and Design at Swinburne University of Technology, Melbourne, Australia.

Janet Salmons is methods guru for SAGE Methodspace and a free-range scholar and creative through Vision2Lead.

Insider Guides to Success in Academia
Series Editors:
Helen Kara,
Independent Researcher, UK and
Pat Thomson,
The University of Nottingham, UK.

The *Insiders' Guides to Success in Academia* address topics too small for a full-length book on their own, but too big to cover in a single chapter or article. These topics have often been the stuff of discussions on social media, or of questions in our workshops. We designed this series to answer these questions in order to provide practical support for doctoral and early career researchers. It is geared to concerns that many people experience. Readers will find these books to be companions who provide advice and help to make sense of everyday life in the contemporary university.

We have therefore:

(1) Invited scholars with deep and specific expertise to write. Our writers use their research and professional experience to provide well-grounded strategies to particular situations.
(2) Asked writers to collaborate. Most of the books are produced by writers who live in different countries, or work in different disciplines, or both. While it is difficult for any book to cover all the diverse contexts in which potential readers live and work, the different perspectives and contexts of writers goes some way to address this problem.

We understand that the use of the term 'academia' might be read as meaning the university, but we take a broader view. Pat does indeed work in a university, but spent a long time working outside of one. Helen is an independent researcher and sometimes works with universities. Both of us understand academic – or scholarly – work as now being conducted in a range of sites, from museums and the public sector to industry research and development laboratories. Academic work is also often undertaken by networks which bring together scholars in various locations. All of our writers understand that this is the case, and use the term 'academic' in this wider sense.

These books are pocket-sized so that they can be carried around and visited again and again. Most of the books have a mix of examples, stories, and exercises as well as explanation and advice. They are written in a collegial tone, and from a position of care as well as knowledge.

Together with our writers, we hope that each book in the series can make a positive contribution to the work and life of readers, so that you too can become insiders in scholarship.

Helen Kara, PhD FAcSS,
Independent Researcher
https://helenkara.com/
@DrHelenKara (Twitter/Insta)
Pat Thomson PhD PSM FAcSS FRSA
Professor of Education, The University of Nottingham
https://patthomson.net
@ThomsonPat

Books in the series

Publishing from your Doctoral Research
Create and Use a Publication Strategy
Janet Salmons and Helen Kara

'Making it' as a Contract Researcher
A Pragmatic Look at Precarious Work
Nerida Spina, Jess Harris, Simon Bailey and Mhorag Goff

Being Well in Academia
A Practical Companion
Petra Boynton

Reframing and Rethinking Collaboration in Higher Education and Beyond
A Practical Guide for Doctoral Students and Early Career Researchers
Narelle Lemon and Janet Salmons

The Thesis by Publication in the Social Sciences and Humanities
Putting the Pieces Together
Lynn P. Nygaard and Kristin Solli

Reframing and Rethinking Collaboration in Higher Education and Beyond

A Practical Guide for Doctoral Students and Early Career Researchers

Narelle Lemon and Janet Salmons

LONDON AND NEW YORK

First published 2021
by Routledge
2 Park Square, Milton Park, Abingdon, Oxon OX14 4RN

and by Routledge
52 Vanderbilt Avenue, New York, NY 10017

Routledge is an imprint of the Taylor & Francis Group, an informa business

© 2021 Narelle Lemon and Janet Salmons

The right of Narelle Lemon and Janet Salmons to be identified as authors of this work has been asserted by them in accordance with sections 77 and 78 of the Copyright, Designs and Patents Act 1988.

All rights reserved. No part of this book may be reprinted or reproduced or utilised in any form or by any electronic, mechanical, or other means, now known or hereafter invented, including photocopying and recording, or in any information storage or retrieval system, without permission in writing from the publishers.

Trademark notice: Product or corporate names may be trademarks or registered trademarks, and are used only for identification and explanation without intent to infringe.

British Library Cataloguing-in-Publication Data
A catalogue record for this book is available from the British Library

Library of Congress Cataloging-in-Publication Data
A catalog record has been requested for this book

ISBN: 978-0-367-22614-5 (hbk)
ISBN: 978-0-367-22616-9 (pbk)
ISBN: 978-0-429-27599-9 (ebk)

Typeset in Helvetica
by SPi Global, India

Visit the eResources: www.routledge.com/9780367226169

Narelle dedicates this book to those who have inspired a *Circle of Niceness*, and to those looking for their *Circle of Niceness*.

Janet dedicates this book to Hannah, Zac, Alex, Sam, and Oliver, who motivate her to work for a future where people make the effort needed to overcome the boundaries that divide them.

Contents

List of figures — xii
List of tables — xiii
About this book — xiv
About the authors — xxiv
Acknowledgements — xxvii

1. **Collaboration fundamentals** — 1
2. **Collaboration skills and strengths: Thinking about your role** — 23
3. **Collaboration and the PhD experience** — 51
4. **Collaboration skills and strengths: Working as a group** — 75
5. **Collaboration and teaching and learning** — 104
6. **Collaboration and co-research** — 124
7. **Collaborative writing** — 148
8. **Collaboration in the real world: Working through dilemmas of conflict, and inertia** — 167

Appendix I — 180

Index — 186

Figures

Figure 0.1	Janet and Narelle's collaboration journey: The Taxonomy of Collaboration in action!	xviii
Figure 1.1	Collaboration within and across boundaries.	7
Figure 1.2	Taxonomy of Collaboration.	12
Figure 2.1	Project *'let's work together'*: Mind map of embedding the strength of creativity.	33
Figure 2.2	Working collaboratively and building skills and strengths.	39
Figure 3.1	Self-care is worthy of our attention.	52
Figure 4.1	The *Circle of Niceness*.	89
Figure 5.1	Collaborative Knowledge Learning Model.	109
Figure 5.2	Applying the Taxonomy of Collaboration for instruction.	111
Figure 6.1	Collaborative knowledge learning in a research context.	127
Figure 6.2	Crossing disciplinary boundaries.	130
Figure 6.3	Boundary exercise.	146
Figure 7.1	Individual and collective outcomes.	153
Figure 7.2	Mapping collaborative writing process, with individual outcomes.	154
Figure 7.3	Collaborative writing with a parallel work design.	157
Figure 7.4	Collaborative writing with a sequential work design.	158
Figure 7.5	Collaborative writing with a synergistic work design.	159
Figure 7.6	Best practices for collaborative writing.	161

Tables

Table 1.1	Factors for collaborative advantage or inertia	9
Table 1.2	Meet the cases	17
Table 2.1	VIA strengths list – a great starting point to develop a common language	28
Table 2.2	The differences between skills and strengths	32
Table 2.3	Mindfulness presence in supportive and unsupportive collaborations	40
Table 3.1	Mapping our self-care routines	54
Table 3.2	Approaches to relationship support and needs	61
Table 3.3	'Three Cs' of postgraduate study	65
Table 4.1	Thinking and working with others	82
Table 4.2	Communication response matrix	98
Table 5.1	Knowledge dimensions in Bloom's Taxonomy revision	108
Table 5.2	Using conceptual models for instruction	117

About this book

We would like to start by sharing thoughts about collaboration that are at the heart of this book, and the story about how we have collaborated as authors. We utilised many of our ideas that we will explore throughout the book and hope our example encourages you to take a positive and open-minded approach to when you collaborate with others in your academic, professional, and personal life. We hope our example motivates you to apply the practical tips we offer, and supports your further growth as doctoral students and early career researchers.

First, we want to emphasise a few key ideas about how we have framed collaboration. We think it is important to place these premises upfront, before you read about our experience as authors, and engage with the book content. We have written this book to reframe collaboration in a positive way.

Collaboration is essential in most academic and professional work we do. It is dynamic. What works for one situation might not work for another, because whenever people are involved individual characteristics and preferences are at play. Consideration is required for varying discipline expectations, unwritten rules, communication styles, hierarchy, organisational cultures and settings, power differentials, involvement with external key stakeholders, needs, experience, lived experiences, and parameters vary depending on whether you are working across research, writing, learning and teaching, policy or leadership. These factors are also layered with your own energy levels, mental health, career stage, confidence, personality, work ethic, cultural background, or epistemological viewpoints. It is complex! We hope you can grasp the flexible and complicated nature of collaboration before applying what will work best for you, and indeed what will work best for you in different circumstances.

Is it collaboration or a group effort?

We begin this book by defining the term, because, as is the case with other trendy terms, *collaboration* is overused. What we have noticed is that there is often a misunderstanding when any work that involves someone else is called a collaboration. The fact that we are working together does not mean we are *collaborating*. Collaboration occurs when we share a commitment to a goal, and achieve the goal together in ways we could not accomplish on our own. True collaboration goes beyond merely cooperating with others, and it is this *going beyond* that makes collaboration unique in human endeavours.

There are different types of collaborations. We underpin this with a Taxonomy of Collaboration (Salmons, 2019) which is used to frame discussion of processes and stages of collaboration discussed throughout the book. Our approach to writing this book demonstrates how the Taxonomy of Collaboration (Salmons, 2019) looks in action, and we will uncover this shortly. The taxonomy is introduced in Chapter 1 and used as a framework to explain processes and work designs associated with successful collaborative projects. This taxonomy suggests three fundamental ways in which collaborative partners organise work, and points out how the processes of mindful reflection, dialogue, and constructive review are used when individuals collaborate.

We hope our writing reveals the multiple layers to collaboration in ways that help you move past previous assumptions and consider new or ongoing projects more carefully. We invite you to begin to notice more, to be present and aware of ways you and partners engage when planning, conducting, and assessing collaborative work. We invite you to reframe and rethink.

Overcoming negative assumptions with collaboration

We acknowledge that too often discussions about collaboration in higher education are focused on the negative – what went wrong, who is a problem, how to problem solve difficult situations, not having a choice, impact of the massification and commodification, and sadly, on many occasions, how someone has been 'broken' (you know those too common experiences centred around erosion of the academic profession where competitiveness and self-centered approaches take someone else out!). We understand this, we really do, with a heavy heart.

We want to interrupt and push back on negative and destructive reactions to collaboration. As a response to these situations, we support your efforts to make the changes that you can make individually to improve your experiences in collaborative projects. We have written this book from a positive and appreciative perspective. The book is informed by theory, original research, and proven strategies. We are reframing collaboration in higher education. We want to empower you to move from a focus on 'I' to an embrace of the 'we', and 'us'.

Our journey as co-authors

Figure 0.1 is a visual representation of our journey throughout this book project. You can see how we moved through the Taxonomy of Collaboration stages throughout the project. We worked virtually, embracing platforms that allowed us to move between the parallel, sequential, and synergistic work designs as specified in the Taxonomy of Collaboration. We share our journey so you can see an example of how two people could cross the globe virtually to form a productive and fruitful collaboration. This project has allowed us to form not only a professional relationship but also a personal friendship.

Both of us have had extensive collaborative experience within, outside, and across numerous higher education and industry contexts, in projects, both large and small, that entailed conducting research, writing, learning and teaching, and policy-making. We have led, been co-leaders, and been team members. We have had wonderful experiences, and just as many that were not.

When we came together, we didn't know each other. We had never met. Janet lives in Boulder, Colorado in the USA and Narelle in Melbourne, Australia. We had not crossed paths, nor did we know of each other. We were brought together by a mutual colleague and friend, Helen Kara (one of the co-editors of this book series). Helen knows both of us very well, from working with each of us over a number of years. Helen identified our strengths, skills, and interests and had the idea that joining us together would provide a unique collaboration. And, ironically, Helen invited us to write about collaboration!

We are at different career points with different disciplinary focuses, but we discovered we have many similar interests and shared values. We talked about these core

xviii *About this book*

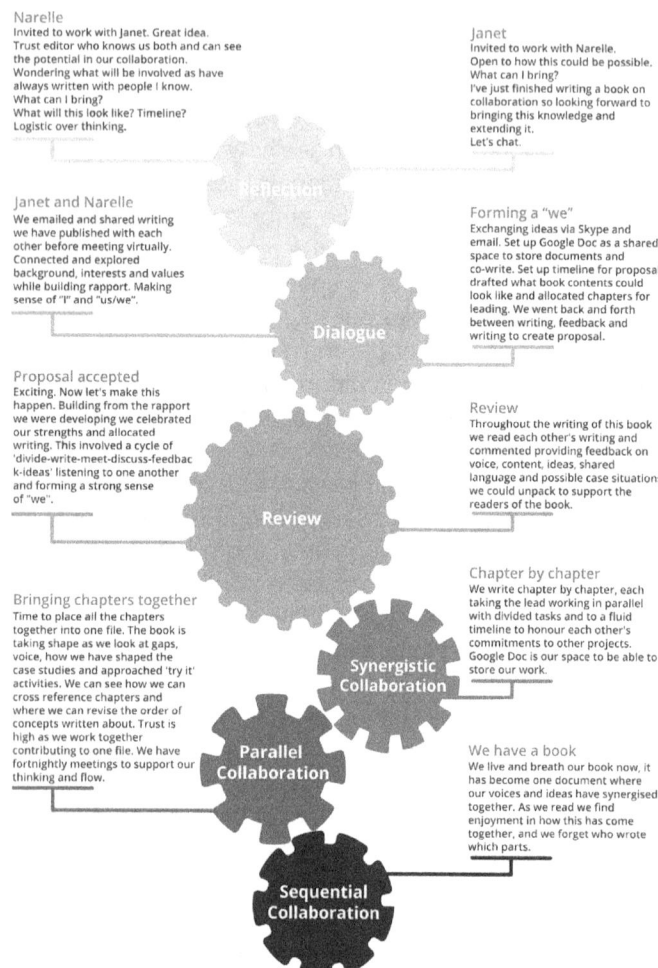

Figure 0.1 Janet and Narelle's collaboration journey: The Taxonomy of Collaboration in action!

principles before agreeing to work on this book. What was it we each valued in collaboration? This was important not only for working together but also because this is the topic we were to write about. We talked openly about these aspects in order to develop a rapport and to investigate how we could move from being 'I' to 'We/Us'.

As discussed in Chapter 2, Narelle's strengths are: creativity, curiosity, honesty, humility, leadership, and persistence, whereas Janet's are: zest, curiosity, love, gratitude, appreciation of beauty and excellence, and creativity. Our shared strengths – honesty, persistence, zest and curiosity enabled us to recognise and celebrate our collaborative partnership.

Creativity is the skill set and mindset that shone for us as partners – we thrived on thinking about how we could inspire others to experience successful collaborations. Outside this book project, we are both deeply involved and enriched by our work in the arts. To apply these interests in practical ways, we were motivated to create tables and figures throughout the book that highlight different aspects and support your connection to concepts. We also both love to write, so our creativity was put into action in developing this book.

We note that while our connection came naturally, many of you reading this book might not have had this experience. We recognise that collaboration can be difficult, and that, as new graduates and early career researchers, the stakes are high. So, we share our experience as a way to empower you to think about how you can approach collaborations from a positive perspective. Beginning with your strengths and values is something that is important, and we encourage you to make time for this foundational step. In Chapters 2 and 4, you will find detailed discussions about self-awareness and both individual and group processes that can help you recognise, understand, and work from your strengths. In Chapter 3, we look at these issues in the context of doctoral student life.

As we have worked, we have been in constant contact. We have made time for each other to connect but also to honour thinking, writing, feedback, and the processing of ideas. We have embraced change and flexibility.

As we have negotiated the project, we have enacted the *Circle of Niceness*. You will learn about the *Circle of Niceness* in Chapter 4. As per that model, we have listened deeply, enjoyed each other's company and we have shared insights.

Throughout this process of collaboration, we have been mindful, aware with attitude, attention and intention. We have had times when we have both had conflicting deadlines and have worked together with an awareness to be honest and open about this. We've asked the questions:

- What can I do to support you?
- Is there another way in which we can approach this?
- What is the best approach for us right now?

And we've been flexible about making changes to accommodate each other.

We have thought about different contexts, different experiences, and different stages of working in higher education and the field at large. And we have embodied attention and an attitude that is both honest but also helpful. We have problem-solved, pondered, and pushed each other through deadlines and hurdles while also celebrating moments. Our trust has grown. We acknowledge that a collaboration involving two partners is simpler than one that includes a large, complex, diverse membership. We fully realise that some collaborative partners confront intractable problems, and face obstacles beyond their control. We close the book with a chapter about ways to work through, or with, such issues and keep going.

We moved from not knowing one another, to learning about one another, through to becoming a 'we' and this book is the result. It showcases each of our interests, but also culminates in a text that we hope will help you, our readers.

Scope of the book

This book is not and cannot be everything to everyone. So, let's connect with what we do not do.

Given the length of this book, it was not possible to address all options or situations. We do not address specifics of writing papers, developing tools, researching with public institutions, working with the media, differences in collaborations (organisations, teams, departments, etc.), how to approach someone about a potential collaboration, how to reach out to researchers from other disciplines, cultures, or countries, offer charts and proformas, legal requirements, how to form budgets, collaborating with funders, working in unionised environments, or collaborating with volunteers. These are important but would cover several books in themselves. We believe if you do not have the basics of who you are, what you bring, or how to establish productive collaborations the aforementioned areas will not function anyway.

Over to YOU! No matter if you are a doctoral student or an early career researcher, before we let you explore the content of this book and engage with the ideas, we want to connect with you on one further aspect of how to read this book. We have mentioned that we explore key aspects of collaboration through a positive lens, to inspire the change that can be possible, and is required. Throughout this approach we are encouraging you to make deliberate decisions about how you are going to approach collaborations and how you wish to engage with others. We want you to make careful and considerate decisions. You are invited to consider how you have strengths in some areas, and in other areas that will grow, or be complemented by a collaborative partner (or partners).

Whether you are at the beginning of collaboration or in the midst of a challenging collaborative research project or collaborative teaching and learning situation, we want to inspire you to be aware, to be reflect. We invite you to reconsider the importance of practices such as knowing your 'why', being aware of your strengths, knowing how to approach someone who has a different strength or approach from you, and why your wellbeing and self-care are critical throughout this process. We want to present these ideas to you and to encourage you to consider the *how* to actually implement them.

As you read we invite to think about:

- What kind of relationship do I want with my collaborators?
- What strengths do I have? How can I complement these with partners, or use them to assist the work I do myself and with others? How are these approached differently according to the context?
- What kind of reframing do I need to do?
- What assumptions have I made about myself, others, or even what I think a collaboration is?
- Where is my place in a collaboration? How does my role change across collaborations or within a collaboration? What do I need to (re)think through?

– How can I continue to grow in my approach to collaboration? What do I notice in myself within different collaborations across varying situations and contexts?

We intended to create a book that is open, honest, and insightful. We share it as a starting point for your study and practice, to inspire and fuel how you can approach collaboration at any stage of your journey. We hope you enjoy reading it and that it motivates and inspires you to create collaborative moments. We hope the impact will extend to those you work with and those who will read your work. Please pass on your learning and embrace new ways of working. We wish you well as you explore collaboration and create possibilities.

As you engage with this book, keep in contact. Share your insights, ask your questions. We are fascinated to know how you use this book and what possibilities are enacted for you. You can connect with us:

Book website: www.exploreandcreateco.com/reframing-and-rethinking-collaboration-in-higher-education
Twitter: @rellypops and @einterview
Instagram: @rellypops and @exploreandcreateco

About the authors

Narelle Lemon, DEd, MEd, BMus, BTeach, DipMan, MAPP (Melb) is an Associate Professor in Education located in the Department of Education, Faculty of Health, Arts and Design at Swinburne University of Technology, Melbourne, Australia. Narelle's overarching research area is focused on participation and engagement. She explores this through a variety of avenues, including: social media use for learning and professional development; creativity and arts education; and positive psychology specifically aimed at mindful practice and coping strategies. She is interested in the lived experience of being an academic – especially in the areas of care, collaboration, and mindful and supportive practices. This has been explored through online identity with social media and the projects called *Academics Who Tweet* and *Reach and Engagement: Social Media Use By Artists, Art Educators, Academics*, and also through books such as *Being "In and Out": Providing voice to early career women in academia* (2014), and a co-edited book *The Mindful Scholar: Practices and Perspectives* (2018). She has also transferred her work in mindfulness with a co-authored book with Cambridge University Press called *Building Mindful Resources as Pre--Service Teacher: Strategies for Professional Experience* (2020).

Narelle has received over $1.2 million worth of nationally competitive grants and awards. She has been successfully awarded research awards, including: La Trobe University Mid-Career Researcher Excellence Award (2016); La Trobe University Early Career Researcher Excellence Award (2013);

Early Career Supervisor with Most Publications Award within the School of Education, RMIT University (2012); and Early Career Researcher International Travel Award from RMIT Research and Innovation (2012). In 2020 was awarded a 2019 Citation for Outstanding Contributions to Student Learning, as part of the Australian Award for University Teaching (AAUT) program for her sustained and innovative work with social media integration in learning and teaching within higher education and industry for professional development.

She is often invited as an expert speaker and commentator in the media and for online communities on wellbeing and self-care, research culture, and education issues. Narelle blogs at *Chat with Rellypops* and *Exploreandcreateco.com*, Tweets and Instagram's as *@Rellypops*, and curates an online project to promote self-care in the everyday on Instagram through *@exploreandcreateco*.

Janet Salmons, PhD is the Methods Guru and lead writer for SAGE Methodspace and a free-range scholar and creative through Vision2Lead. Her areas of interest include emerging research methods, and teaching and collaborative learning in the digital age. Her most recent books are: *What Kind of Researcher Are You?* (2020); *Publishing from your Doctoral Research: Create and Use a Publication Strategy* (2020); *Learning to Collaborate, Collaborating to Learn* (2019); *Find the Theory in Your Research* (2019); *Getting Data Online* (2019); and *Doing Qualitative Research Online* (2016).

Dr. Salmons served on the doctoral faculty of the Capella University School of Business from 1999 to 2016, and was honored with the Harold Abel Distinguished Faculty Award for 2011–2012 and the Steven Shank Recognition for Teaching in 2012, 2013, 2014, 2015 and 2016.

Dr. Salmons received a BS in Adult and Community Education from Cornell University; an MA in Social Policy Studies from SUNY Empire State College, and a PhD in Interdisciplinary Studies and Educational Leadership at the Union Institute & University.

She is an honorary member of the TAA Council of Fellows (2019) and received the Mike Keedy Award (2018) in recognition of enduring service to authors. She lives and works in Boulder, Colorado.

Acknowledgements

Narelle acknowledges the opportunities she has had throughout her career to learn how to collaborate and learn from others. She is especially appreciative of the collaboration with Janet, which has been a magical experience filled with hope, love, care, and inspiration. It has been an honour Janet, thank you.

Janet acknowledges the lessons learned from colleagues who have demonstrated the power and potential of collaboration. She appreciates the opportunity to work with Narelle on a journey from stranger to trusted friend.

We thank Giannis Misiakos for his designs that feature throughout the book with the case study avatars and at Figure 0.1, 2.1, 3.1, and 4.1.

1 Collaboration fundamentals

What will you learn by studying this chapter?

This chapter introduces collaboration in relation to higher education by positioning it in the areas of student, academic, and professional life related to research, and learning and teaching. An overview of what collaboration is, why it is important, how it operates, and how it is relevant to the work we do as doctoral students and academics lays the foundation for the ideas and recommendations offered throughout the book.

In this chapter you will gain an understanding of:

- Collaboration definitions.
- Why collaboration is important for students and those beginning their careers.
- Questions to consider when determining ways to work within and across boundaries.
- Ways to think through aspects of a project using the Taxonomy of Collaboration.

The big picture: What is collaboration?

The word *collaborate* has its origins in the Latin word *collaborare*, 'to work together' (OED, 2005). The importance of 'working together' has increased in recent decades. In today's high-performance world collaboration typically involves more than simply the enjoyment and sense of shared accomplishment derived from 'working together'. There must also be some demonstrable value that merits commitment of time and resources to a collaborative team, project or partnership. Barbara Gray has defined collaboration in a way that emphasises the interdependence of players:

> [Collaboration is] a process through which parties who see different aspects of a problem can constructively explore their differences and search for solutions that go beyond their own limited vision of what is possible ... Collaboration establishes a give and take among the stakeholders that is designed to produce solutions that none of them working independently could achieve.
>
> (Gray, 1989, p. 11)

Gray elaborated on this definition in a later study with Wood: according to them, collaboration occurs when 'a group of autonomous stakeholders of an problem domain engage in an interactive process, using shared rules, norms, and structures to act or decide on issues related to that domain' (Wood & Gray, 1991, p. 437). In a further refinement, Kanter distinguishes between *collaboration*, which is characterised by 'creating value together,' and *exchange*, which is characterised by 'getting something back for what you put in' (Kanter, 1994, p. 97).

The definition we will use encompasses these characteristics:

> Collaboration is an interactive process that engages two or more partners who work together to achieve value and outcomes they could not accomplish independently.
> (Salmons, 2019, p. 5)

Let's parse this definition. First, collaboration is an interactive process. When people interact, they aim for mutuality and reciprocity. It is a process, not an end unto itself. Second, collaboration involves two or more people who work together. We will use the term *partners* to indicate participation in and commitment to the collaboration. Third, the interactive process and work lead to outcomes that are different from those that individuals can accomplish on their own. Implicit in this definition is a view that collaboration is not a single activity, but a set of interrelated processes, steps, and work designs.

Outcomes of the collaborative process can be either *individual* or *collective*. We may complete parts of a project independently and integrate our efforts to achieve a shared goal. We generate one outcome that represents all of our work: a collective outcome. Or, we might collaborate with others for social learning and exchange of ideas, but create outcomes on our own: an individual outcome.

How does collaboration work?

Sometimes we know someone, perhaps from taking a class together. We share research interests and professional goals. We get along well and enjoy each other's company. When one of us says, 'Why don't we work on a project together?' the other readily agrees. We jump right into brainstorming and define what we want to do, and how we will move forward. Our enthusiasm is contagious, and we are each intrinsically motivated to be creative and generous when it comes to the effort we are willing to put into this project. When we share drafts with each other, we are confident about receiving respectful and constructive feedback. If one of us encounters a problem or there is a delay, the other understands and makes adjustments because we trust each other. We are able to give and take, build on each other's strengths and fill in for each other's shortcomings. When we complete the project, we are ready to celebrate, knowing we've accomplished something that melds the unique contributions we each made to the project.

In other situations, we have little choice about who the collaborative partners are, how many are involved, or the nature of the project we are expected to complete together. The project may have been determined by people at another level of the institution who lack understanding of the day-to-day practicalities. Perhaps collaborative partners are assigned because funding was predicated on the participation of multiple stakeholders. Assigned collaborative partners share an interest in the project, but their diverse disciplinary and/or cultural backgrounds mean we approach questions from very different perspectives, and perhaps use different terminology to describe them. Some or all will be working virtually, across multiple time zones. Our expectations about showing up for meetings or the timely delivery of work in progress are not always met. When it is time to share drafts, we are uneasy about an uncertain process. Because we are worried that we will be penalised for others' inadequacies, trust in the collaborative project and partners begins to erode.

We are likely to encounter these and other kinds of circumstances where some factors associated with a collaborative effort are in our control, and others are not. We have fun working with others when engaged at an individual level among group members with whom we share familiar frames of reference and a level of trust. In such collaborative projects we can work with the natural flow and succeed without having formal protocols in place. However, once we add in more complexity, agreements, timelines, checkpoints, and systems of accountability are needed. This book is designed to help you navigate and negotiate in situations where the collaboration is complex and the stakes for success are high.

Collaborating within and across boundaries

Knowledge is the first step towards overcoming problems. Once we understand potential pitfalls, we can find ways to work with or around them. When we are collaborating across boundaries, we need to allow adequate time to determine shared goals and plans. Let's look at a few reasons why this is the case.

If I said the following statement to you, you might respond in a few different ways.

> Let's propose a PDW about SDGs for AOM next year! Maybe SIM would be interested.

If you are interested in the Sustainable Development Goals and you are a member of the Academy of Management, you are familiar with professional development workshops that are part of the annual conference and you know that Social Issues in Management is one division. We could get right to work on our proposal because we would understand the steps involved. If you are not involved with these efforts, you might be confused or alienated by this request. If I made the suggestion to a group, and you are the only one who was unfamiliar with these efforts, you might feel you don't belong as a part of this collaboration.

When we collaborate within our own organisations or institutions, we have a common understanding about an overarching mission, decision-making structures, organisational culture, and the protocols involved with different kinds of projects. We know the acronyms and lingo, and we know who to talk with to get things done. Similarly, when we collaborate within our own disciplines or fields of study, we share foundations and ways of thinking. In contrast, when we work across boundaries, we need to define our terms and our ways of working before we can collaborate effectively. Leadership in inter-group contexts differs from that in intra-group ones due to greater complexity, and the lack of common hierarchy for decision-making. Working across groups we discover multiple ways in which individuals can 'make things happen' in different group contexts (Vangen & Diamond, 2016).

Figure 1.1 illustrates collaboration within or across boundaries. This Venn diagram helps us reflect on the common factors we share within a given group, and how we might identify our boundaries.

Think about the boundaries you are willing and unwilling to cross. What commonalities can you build on in order to work together successfully? Think about how you would define the organisations, disciplines, groups, or cultures within which you might feel comfortable collaborating. What agreements will you need to feel at ease about collaborating?

Collaboration fundamentals

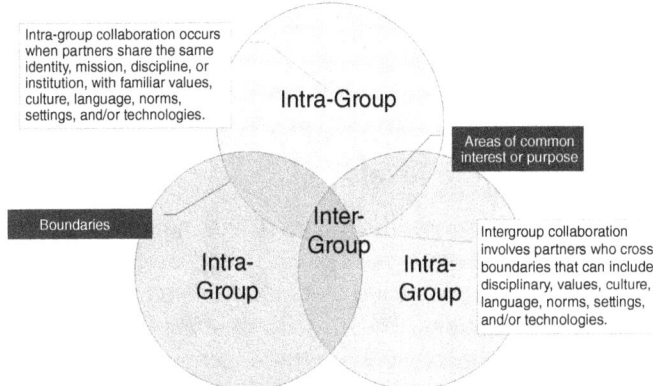

Figure 1.1 Collaboration within and across boundaries.

Advantage or inertia?

Chris Huxham and Siv Vangen have researched collaboration extensively. They identified a tension between two forces, which they termed *collaborative advantage* and *collaborative inertia* (Huxham & Vangen, 2005; Vangen, 2017, 2019; Vangen & Huxham, 2012). Collaborative advantage describes the positive and productive process referred to in our definition. Other researchers describe collaborative advantage in terms of policy-making, value creation, innovation, and capacity for collective action (Dej, 2019; Hansen & Nohria, 2004; Kouzes & Posner, 2002). When we can achieve outcomes and actions that are impossible to accomplish on our own, we have put collaborative advantage to work.

According to Huxham and Vangen, to accomplish collaborative advantage, we need to recognise and address the force of collaborative inertia. Collaborative inertia refers to factors that impede progress or obstruct collaborations from achieving desired outcomes.

Advantage or inertia at the meta, meso, or micro levels

Let's look at some of the factors at the meta, meso, and micro levels that enable or obstruct successful collaboration. For our purposes, the *meta* level refers to societal or global collaborations. The *meso* level refers to the organisational group level, such as the educational institution, research institute, or department. The meso level could also refer to professional or research disciplines, and related societies or associations. The *micro* level refers to factors at the individual level.

Collaborations can occur either within a single level or across multiple levels and boundaries. For example, a collaboration between universities, government agencies, and non-governmental organisations (NGOs) in different countries crosses multiple boundaries and operates at the meta level. A collaboration between departments in the same university crosses fewer boundaries and operates at a meso level. A collaboration between individuals may or may not cross boundaries and operates at the micro level. A collaboration across levels could include involve consultants from an outside agency and a university department. Table 1.1 shows some factors. Use Exercise 1, described at the end of the chapter, to make notes about your own experiences and observations.

Ideally, the meso, meta, and micro levels align to further the collaboration. When our cultural mores celebrate the value of the group, collective work is appreciated.

Table 1.1 Factors for collaborative advantage or inertia

	Factors that support collaborative advantage	Factors that enable collaborative inertia
Meta	Cultures where community and group success are celebrated	Cultures where individualism is celebrated
		Laws and regulations that protect proprietary information without exceptions for educational or non-profit/NGO uses
	Disciplines, fields, or professions based on openness and innovation	Disciplines, fields, or professions that have a reputation for being superior to others, or have specialised terminology and approaches not commonly used by others
Meso	Leaders look for opportunities to link efforts with other entities within or across sectors	Leaders cut the institution or organisation off from collaborative partnerships
	Buy-in from management or administration	Obstruction or mixed messages from management or administration
	Modelling by leaders, examples of shared leadership	Top-down leadership and decision-making
	Policies that encourage multiple stakeholder involvement in decision-making and practices	
	Transparency and open communication allowed for internal support and exchange across departments and workgroups	Silos that mean it is difficult to find the expertise needed to complete the project

(Continued)

Table 1.1 Continued

	Factors that support collaborative advantage	Factors that enable collaborative inertia
	Enough time is made available for the establishment of a new collaborative work group. Department chairs or managers emphasise the importance of making plans and clear agreements before proceeding with the new collaborative project.	Participants in the collaborative project to not have the time or leadership needed to establish the necessary agreements, timelines, checkpoints, and plans.
Micro	Open mindset, willingness to work with new people from outside of own disciplinary or social group	Lack of trust in others, lack of confidence that others will share commitment to project
	Manners based in fairness and respect	Win – lose or competitive styles of interacting
	'We're in this together' ethic	Ethic of individualism
	Generosity	Unwillingness to help others
		Unwillingness to seek input or learn from others
	Mindful and reflective attitudes that allow us to make sense of and learn from the collaborative experience	Critical attitudes, blaming others rather than trying to understand them

When leaders create policies in support of cooperation and respect, individuals feel they will be rewarded fairly for their contributions, and collaboration thrives. In cases where cultural mores celebrate the value of the individual, we can feel we are swimming upstream when we try to get things done as a group. We may be doing work together that we know is right, but it will not be adequately recognised or rewarded. Since in the real world we are not likely to find the ideal situation, we need to learn ways to understand and work within our cultural norms and circumstances.

Putting process and organisation together: A Taxonomy of Collaboration

Let's go back to the definition again:

> Collaboration is an interactive **process** that engages two or more partners who **work together** to achieve value and outcomes they could not accomplish independently.
> (Salmons, 2019, p. 5)

Two concepts are highlighted here: *process* and *working together*. Throughout this book we will use the Taxonomy of Collaboration shown in Figure 1.2 to help us think through the specific processes we use when we collaborate, and the ways we allocate tasks when we work together.

The first three parts of the taxonomy refer to interrelated processes essential to success. These processes are: *reflection*, *dialogue*, and *review*.

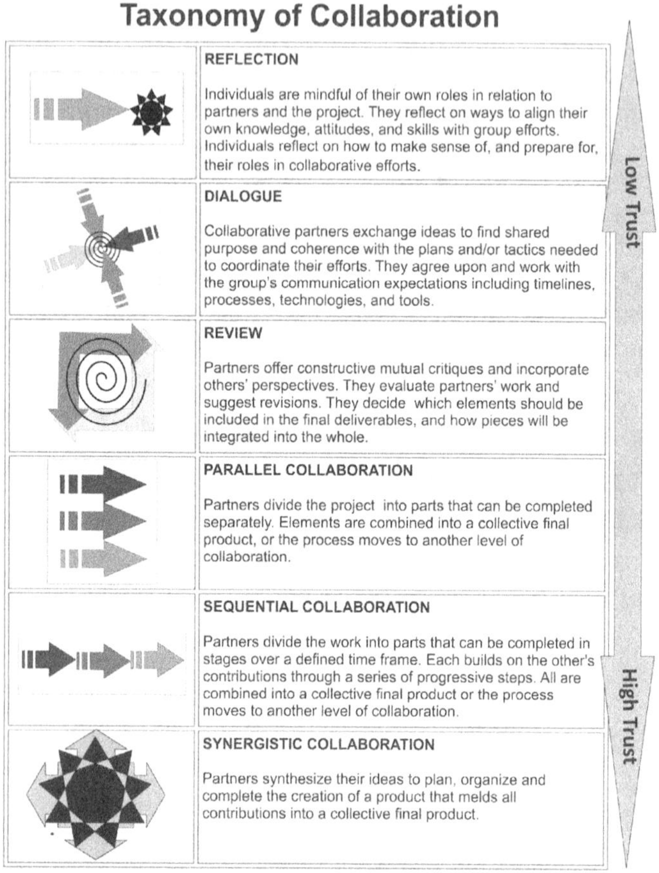

12 *Collaboration fundamentals*

Taxonomy of Collaboration

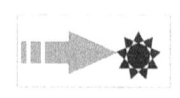	**REFLECTION** Individuals are mindful of their own roles in relation to partners and the project. They reflect on ways to align their own knowledge, attitudes, and skills with group efforts. Individuals reflect on how to make sense of, and prepare for, their roles in collaborative efforts.
	**DIALOGUE** Collaborative partners exchange ideas to find shared purpose and coherence with the plans and/or tactics needed to coordinate their efforts. They agree upon and work with the group's communication expectations including timelines, processes, technologies, and tools.
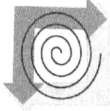	**REVIEW** Partners offer constructive mutual critiques and incorporate others' perspectives. They evaluate partners' work and suggest revisions. They decide which elements should be included in the final deliverables, and how pieces will be integrated into the whole.
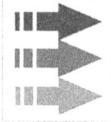	**PARALLEL COLLABORATION** Partners divide the project into parts that can be completed separately. Elements are combined into a collective final product, or the process moves to another level of collaboration.
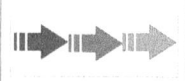	**SEQUENTIAL COLLABORATION** Partners divide the work into parts that can be completed in stages over a defined time frame. Each builds on the other's contributions through a series of progressive steps. All are combined into a collective final product or the process moves to another level of collaboration.
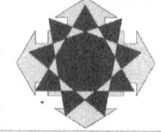	**SYNERGISTIC COLLABORATION** Partners synthesize their ideas to plan, organize and complete the creation of a product that melds all contributions into a collective final product.

(Low Trust at top → High Trust at bottom)

c. Vision2Lead 2005-2020

Figure 1.2 Taxonomy of Collaboration.

First, we need to mindfully reflect on our own roles and contributions to the project. We need to make sense of our experiences in relation to our partners as well as the project itself. We need to be self-aware and cognisant of differences and boundaries that might make us feel uncomfortable.

Second, we need to be able to communicate with collaborative partners. We need to communicate in order to establish goals and expectations for our work with collaborative partners. We need to define terms and understand others' ways of making decisions, framing issues, and getting things done. In the digital age, some or all of this communication might occur electronically. This means we need Internet access, digital literacy, and availability the same software tools.

Third, we need to be able to give and receive constructive feedback about work in progress. In most collaborative projects we complete some parts individually. We need to release our work to others for input, with the realisation that some of our work may be included in the final project and some may not. Collaborative partners develop review criteria to keep the process positive and productive.

The next three parts of the taxonomy refer to ways we might organise our work. We might simply divide up the project and work on our respective parts in parallel. We might be dividing the project up among individuals, or breaking a large project group into smaller teams. We use the term *parallel collaboration* to describe this way of working.

Another option involves dividing the project up in parts that individuals or small teams complete the work in stages. We use the term *sequence of collaboration* to describe this way of working.

When collaborative partners manage their work using parallel or sequential approaches, they will need to determine a process for organising, editing, and melding the parts into a final deliverable. To do so they will need to use the processes of dialogue and review.

A third option is to work together rather than dividing the project. In this situation, we brainstorm and complete the work as a group. We use the term *synergistic collaboration* to describe this way of working.

This taxonomy does not depict a linear process. Rather, we combine these processes and work designs to meet the needs of the collaborative partners and fit the particular characteristics of the project. For example, a more complex project that crosses multiple boundaries might require more synchronous discussions than a simple collaboration involving individuals who share common foundations of knowledge and ways of operating. The project with higher potential for collaborative inertia will benefit from more thoughtful consideration of work designs. The arrow representing *trust* once across all aspects of the taxonomy because throughout any collaborative process, partners rely on mutual trust in order to achieve shared goals.

Introducing cases and examples

We'll be exploring different scenarios where collaboration will be needed, useful, or required in the next stage of your academic or professional life. To help you think through these various situations, we'll think through how individuals might think through and act on decisions and considerations. Take this opportunity to meet Elizabeth, Phillipe, Jesse, and Alicia (Table 1.2). Do you identify with any of them?

Throughout the coming chapters, we will explore ways that dilemmas and options might play out in the situations Phillipe, Elizabeth, Jesse, and Alicia face in their respective positions.

Phillipe is completing his PhD and also undertaking contract teaching work in a university. He has worked collaboratively with other students on assigned projects where roles and expectations were clearly defined. However, he has not had the occasion to collaborate as a faculty member. In this new role, he will participate in committees and projects with others who are more experienced, and have known each other for many years.

Alicia is a postdoctoral researcher (or a postdoc as this position is often called) in a research institute where she is conducting research on a pre-specified project. Alicia completed her PhD with a panel of supervisors and has just graduated. She is in a temporary position, having just signed a three-year contract funded by a major national funding body with a different university from where she studied, allowing her to continue her training as a researcher and gain skills and experience that will prepare her for her academic career post PhD. However, she is feeling pressure to publish so she can compete for a permanent position.

Elizabeth is an early career researcher who previously worked in her field before returning to university for a PhD. She is now working in an NGO that studies needs and develops new services. She has acknowledged that she needs to build a credible research trajectory within her non-academic job. She has taken accepted the opportunity to work with colleagues who have invited her to be part of a research project, and she is contemplating the possibility of doing some independent research.

Jesse is an early career researcher, having completed a PhD two years ago. They are now working as a lecturer in their first ongoing full-time position. Their role involves teaching, research, and leadership workloads. Jesse is negotiating how they use their time best to work as a collaborator in a professional team on tasks that are aligned to teaching priorities for the university. They are trying to manage a research profile and build an approach that utilises a smart way of working to align their teaching load and initiatives with others across scholarship of learning and teaching.

Table 1.2 Meet the cases

Phillipe	**Alicia**	**Jesse**	**Elizabeth**
PhD student with contract teaching position.	Postdoc on short-term contract.	Early career researcher in full-time position.	Engaged in empirical research outside of academia

Into practice: Why is it important to collaborate in academic and professional life?

We need to collaborate to succeed in almost any academic or professional position. More specifically, we need to know how to organise, plan, manage, and participate in collaborative efforts.

Conducting research and writing

Look at the research books on your shelf and the research articles in your files. How many of them have solo authors? Writing books or scholarly articles is time-consuming, so working with partners means you can share the workload. You can also incorporate a wider range of thinking when you welcome others' insights.

As you move beyond student assignments and into more sophisticated research in academic or professional settings, you will increasingly need to work as a part of the research team. You might take responsibility for some part of the larger investigation and need to follow protocols and expectations set with others. Or you might take the lead on a research project and need to engage others to carry out various parts of the study.

Teaching

Not very long ago, the role of a faculty member in a university was a fairly independent one. Professors were entirely responsible for the development and delivery of their courses. Now even the most traditional institutions offer courses online and through blended approaches where face-to-face classes are complemented with online materials and assignments. Not only are new styles of teaching and learning necessary – the whole process of curriculum and course development has changed. Increasingly, a wide range of people including academic leaders, subject matter experts, editors and copyright coordinators, media developers, assessment specialists, instructional designers and instructional technologists – and faculty – work together to design curricula and courses. In some cases, the curriculum or course may involve more than one disciplinary field, making the development team multi-disciplinary as well as cross-functional. The previously independent faculty member accustomed to following established course routines must now learn to collaborate with diverse professionals – and most likely at least some of the collaborative process will occur online.

Instructional practices are changing as well. Traditional lecture methods of instruction worked as a push approach that treated all students as if they were the same, in contrast to the pull strategy, where students access the material they need when they need it. These shifts mean today's faculty members not only create the environments where students can collaborate, their roles *with* students are also more collaborative.

Offering service to the field in society

Beyond simply getting academic work done, we need to collaborate in order to address the social problems of our time. Most challenging and persistent issues need expertise, experience, and insights drawn from beyond one culture, professional or academic or discipline. For research to have an authentic impact, we need to reach across institutional boundaries to work with those whose lives can be improved by using our research findings.

Take it away

Collaboration engages participants in an interactive process of working together towards a shared purpose. It is important for students, postdocs, or early career researchers to learn skills and attitudes that will help them be successful when they are engaged with collaborative writing, research, and efforts associated with faculty life such as curriculum development or department committees. While collaborative advantage offers the potential for unique outcomes and solutions to otherwise intractable problems, significant obstacles are associated with collaborative inertia. By understanding these potential problems in developing their skills, we can move forward with productive and enjoyable collaborations throughout our professional, academic, and even personal lives.

In this book we will focus our attention on four types of situations that call on students, postdocs, or early career researchers to work collaboratively:

- **Collaborative writing**: We will think about ways to organise writing projects that include one or more partners.
- **Collaborative research**: We will explore ways researchers work together, sometimes as equals and other times in investigations where senior researchers take the lead and novice researchers provide support.
- **Collaborative work as a postdoc or intern**: We will look at opportunities and challenges specific to temporary positions common to new graduates.
- **Collaborative work as a new faculty member**: We will consider ways that new faculty members can be successful as collaborative partners.

In addition to practical tips and recommendations, we will look at how these situations might realistically unfold in situations Phillipe, Alicia, Jesse, and Elizabeth might face. We hope their strategies might help you think through your own situations.

Collaboration fundamentals 21

Try it! Exercises and questions for discussion or reflection

You can find a document with all of the Try it! exercises and questions on the Routledge website for this book. Record responses or customise the exercises to meet your needs.

Reflective questions

Think about a collaborative project you have experienced in a classroom or workplace context:

- Do you think this collaborative project was successful? Why or why not?
- Did you experience collaborative advantage, collaborative inertia, or both?
- Would you describe the partners in this project as people from within a group with shared cultural and disciplinary backgrounds, or did the project cross boundaries?
- If the project crossed boundaries, how did you feel about insiders and outsiders in this project?
- What do you think about your own role and participation? How could you have been a better collaborative partner?

Exercise

1. Imagine a micro-level collaborative writing project involving four partners. What are the first planning steps you'd recommend? What would you discuss at your first meeting?

References

Dej, E. (2019). Building a collaborative advantage: Network governance and homelessness policy-making in Canada. *BC Studies* (203), 165–166.

Gray, B. (1989). *Collaborating: Finding common ground for multiparty problems*. San Francisco: Jossey Bass.

Hansen, M. T., & Nohria, N. (2004). How to build collaborative advantage. *MIT Sloan Management Review*, *46*(1), 22–30.

Huxham, C., & Vangen, S. (2005). *Managing to collaborate: The theory and practice of collaborative advantage*. Oxford: Routledge.

Kanter, R. M. (1994). Collaborative Advantage: The Art of Alliances. *Harvard Business Review, 72*(4), 96–108.

Kouzes, J. M., & Posner, B. Z. (2002). *The leadership challenge* (3rd ed.). San Francisco: Jossey Bass.

OED. (2005). Oxford English Dictionary. Retrieved from http://www.askoxford.com

Salmons, J. (2019). *Learning to collaborate, collaborating to learn*. Sterling, VA: Stylus Publishing, LLC.

Vangen, S. (2017). A meeting of minds. Charity Finance. Retrieved from http://oro.open.ac.uk/53067/

Vangen, S. (2019). Researching inter-organisational collaboration using RO-AR. In: J. Voets, R. Keast, & C. Koliba (Eds.), *Networks and collaboration in the public sector: Essential research approaches, methodologies and analytic tools* (pp. 125–141). London: Routledge.

Vangen, S., & Diamond, J. (2016). Researching leadership for collaborative advantage. Paper presented at *the 3rd Collective leadership workshop: Methodological challenges in collective leadership research*, New York.

Vangen, S., & Huxham, C. (2012). The tangled web: Unraveling the principle of common goals in collaborations. *Journal of Public Administration Research and Theory*, *22*(4), 731.

Wood, D., & Gray, B. (1991). Toward a comprehensive theory of collaboration. *The Journal of Applied Behavioral Science*, *27*(2), 139–162.

2 Collaboration skills and strengths
Thinking about your role

What you will learn by studying this chapter

When we think about working in a collaboration we rarely pause to make time to think explicitly about what we want to achieve from working with others, and indeed how we can grow from the experience. Sometimes we just jump into a project with fellow students, friends, or colleagues and enjoy the shared effort. But too often in the higher education context we are forced together to plan a new subject, or begin with optimistic intentions for a research project but end up not following through with possibilities due to a lack of direction or leadership. In this chapter we want to begin to disrupt these familiar ways of working. We want to invite you to be curious, that is, to be aware and open to what you would like to develop in yourself.

In this chapter you will gain an understanding of:

- How you can consider your role and position as an individual in a collaborative project.
- Strengths-based literature.
- The differences between skills and strengths for collaboration.

- How mindfulness can support the enactment of strengths.
- How a strengths-based approach to collaboration can support the individual and collective partners.

The big picture: Thinking about strengths

Collaboration involves the enactment of both strengths and skills. Often the difference is not addressed in the doctoral and early career researcher experience of collaboration. This chapter focuses on how working collaboratively can support the building of skills and strengths. The difference between these is as follows: skills are learnt behaviours which often do not energise you, but are necessary for the completion of a task; by contrast, strengths energise us and contribute to a sense of flourishing. Strengths and skills are unique to each of us, and they change over time. In a collaborative project our partners' strengths and skills should ideally complement our own. In this chapter we invite you to think about both your skills and strengths in approaching a collaboration.

Do you know your strengths?

Can you think of a time when you were asked about your strengths in the higher education context? Or when beginning to work with others? If you are like us, we would answer 'kind of' to the first question, and 'no' to the others. Isn't this interesting? As we put this book together, we are very much guided by how we can be the best version of our self when working with others. That means we know what our top strengths are (Narelle – Creativity, Curiosity, Honesty, Humility, Leadership, and Persistence, and Janet – Zest, Curiosity, Love, Gratitude, Appreciation of Beauty and Excellence, and Creativity) and what we bring to working with others. Over the years working in higher education we have become more aware of our strengths. And for Narelle her work in positive psychology has revealed that there is a language available that helps us understand what these are and how to describe them.

Put simply, strengths are something you are good at and enjoy doing. Put academically, strengths are the 'characteristics of a person that allow them to perform well or at their personal best' (Wood et al., 2011, p. 15). Strengths are patterns of thinking, feeling, and behaving that, when exercised, will excite you, engage you, and energise you. They allow you to perform at an optimal level and help you grow as an individual. They are, as Narelle puts it, what make you jump out of bed in the morning excited and ready to go. When working with your strengths, and in consideration for collaborations, a strengths-based approach allows us to flourish. We can see opportunity as a way to grow and build capacity.

A strengths-based approach does not ignore what can be perceived as weaknesses but focuses on and builds from our strengths. When working with a strengths-based perspective we are 'looking for what is working well, how individuals are leveraging strengths, [and] seeking optimal performance' (Oades, Steger, Delle Fave, & Passmore, 2017, p. 2). In this way this is juxtaposed to traditional approaches of working individually and collectively in which a focus can be placed on what is wrong, what someone cannot do; this can be more accurately described as a deficit-based approach. By framing ourselves and the work with others in terms of strengths the aim is to approach the experience with a positive lens, rather than escape or avoid the negative or focus on the negative, what is wrong and how something is not working (Louis & Lopez, 2014; Oades et al., 2017). It doesn't mean we ignore such weaknesses; rather, we reframe and embrace a growth mindset (Dweck, 2017). It is an approach that can support a terminology and/or common language to work with others, and indeed yourself, and a way that is manifested in relationship with others, thus not in isolation.

Strengths-based collaboration

When approaching collaborations through a strengths-based approach we move beyond labelling and extend interactions plus our own learning with a focus on the how (Louis & Lopez, 2014). We acknowledge the potential for inertia, as described in Chapter 1, but frame our studies on the potential for collaborative advantage.

Working with our strengths places a positive energy around what it is we are doing and who we are working with. When working with strengths we are able to form a clear understanding of what is best in people, so that we are viewed as 'who we are' (a part of our core identity) rather than our talents (what we do well), interests (what we enjoy doing), skills (proficiencies we develop), or resources (external support(s)) (Niemiec, 2014).

It is interesting to note that research indicates that most people will identify their weaknesses quicker than their strengths, and that they struggle to describe or share stories that bring their strengths to life (Lopez et al., 2015). So, it may come as no surprise that it has been found that burnout or lowered job satisfaction and motivation are connected to those who do not invest their strengths (McGovern & Miller, 2008; Niemiec, 2014). Does this resonate with you? It does for us.

If you are interested academically to know more about strengths, we will do a little rundown of strengths-based approaches. There are a number of approaches to thinking about and classifying strengths, including Gallup Clifton Strengths Finder, Values-in-Action (VIA) classification of character virtues and strengths (Peterson & Seligman, 2004), the Search Institute's 40 Developmental Assets, and the Strength Profiler (Linley, 2008). All were developed for different reasons, but they are currently used for similar purposes; that is to identify individuals' strengths from a Western perspective (Lopez et al., 2015).

Reflecting on strengths with the VIA Character Strengths tool

One of the most commonly used strengths tools is VIA Character Strengths (VIA, 2018), which uses a 240-item self-report measure, commonly administered online (accessed here: http://bit.ly/2D0deH3), with participants receiving feedback about their top five signature strengths and the ranked priorities of the other 19 strengths. This is a great way to connect with your strengths and may even help you identify what they are for you right now. It can provide you with insights and a common language to work in this way. And this will be the list of strengths we will refer to throughout the book (Table 2.1).

Chris Peterson and Martin Seligman (2004), in developing this tool, set up several criteria which demonstrate how strengths are the route through we which we achieve virtues in our life. Seligman is viewed as the founder of the

Table 2.1 VIA strengths list – a great starting point to develop a common language (VIA Institute on Character, 2018)

Creativity	Curiosity	Judgement	Perspective	Bravery	Perseverance
Zest	Honesty	Social intelligence	Kindness	Love	Leadership
Fairness	Teamwork	Forgiveness	Love of Learning	Gratitude	Spirituality
Self-regulation	Humility	Appreciation of beauty	Prudence	Hope	Humour

positive psychology movement and his work with Peterson has been instrumental in how strengths can be influential in working in ways that make you feel fulfilled and invigorated. Strengths can move, and shift based on life experiences over time, so it is recommended that you take the survey on an annual basis. And as more research is revealed in this area, strengths have been identified as critical for team performance, especially collaborations (McQuaid & Lawn, 2014; Peterson & Seligman, 2004). In this way, strengths for collaboration influence enhanced work engagement and performance (Biswas-Diener, Kashdan, & Lyubchik, 2017; Hodges & Asplund, 2010; van Woerkom & Meyers, 2015) and indicates that the personal strengths lead to healthy work outcomes by promoting increased vitality, concentration, and passionate dedication to work-related tasks (Dubreuil, Forest, & Courcy, 2014) and a greater sense of work satisfaction (Peterson, Stephens, Park, Lee, & Seligman, 2009). This in turn promotes positive and effective collaborations (Green, McQuaid, Purtell, & Dulagil, 2017; Roffey, 2017) and can support the development of a positive culture that embraces individual and collective strengths.

Mindfulness and strengths

There are many noteworthy definitions of mindfulness. For the purpose of this book, however, mindfulness follows the definition of the founder of Western-based interventions, Jon Kabat-Zinn (1994, p. 4) as 'paying attention in a particular way: on purpose, in the present moment, non-judgmentally'. As such, there are two parts to mindfulness. The first is learning to focus attention on one thing, and then being able to bring the attention back when the mind gets distracted. The second part is about the attitude you bring to paying attention – being open, non-judging, and curious about what you are focusing on. Mindfulness can serve as a process that supports awareness of strengths and enhance the practice of character strengths opening up new ways of growth for one (Niemiec et al., 2012, Niemiec, 2014).

Mindfulness opens up exploration for self-improvement (Niemiec, 2014). This is seen as a way to expand our views of our self. Being mindful assists in being able to build on strengths through awareness. Mindfulness offers the *how* for the practice of strengths – that is, to be intentional (Niemiec, 2014). The integration of mindfulness with strengths practice allows for us to become more aware of not only negative/troubling thoughts and feelings but also positive thoughts, emotions, and behaviours (Niemiec, 2014). When in a mindful state we are self-aware, present, we slow down, and are curious and in a neutral attitude. Thus, non-judgmentally we are present in the moment. And when in the moment we create and cultivate experiences that support clear connections to understanding our own wellness, first individually but then as a collective and within different environments. By being present we can connect to experiences that support our strengths and potentially allow us to flourish. Throughout this book we will refer to mindfulness alongside the Taxonomy of Collaboration, because attention to collaborative processes and presence with the project are beneficial to us and to our partners.

In a mindful state we become more in tune with the moment in time, and not preoccupied with stories or elaboration. Through greater self-awareness comes an ability to be able of our own actual/ideal discrepancy, attributes/strengths, barriers/blockers, and repeated patterns. There is a magical ability to be able to pause before reacting and gain perspective in order to be able to connect with others in regard to their feelings, emotions, and behaviours. There is a less reactionary response to situations as mindful skills are learnt and integrated as awareness develops.

Looking closer at strengths and skills

Strengths have been broadly defined as ways of behaving, thinking, or feeling that an individual has a natural capacity for, enjoys doing, and which allow the individual to achieve optimal functioning while they pursue valued outcomes (Govindji & Linley, 2007; Linley & Harrington, 2006; Louis & Lopez, 2014). Strengths energise us (Louis & Lopez, 2014; Waters, 2017), especially when we are tuning into those that help us grow, and when used productively contribute to our development and meeting our goals. Strengths are a part of who we are and are embodied. Skills, on the other hand, are character traits. They are closely connected to our ability to learn to do something that makes you, for example be a good employee; to be an early career researcher or doctoral student in the case of this book. They help you address your day-to-day activities and build your professional know-how. You perform skills daily in order to successfully address your workload and job responsibilities well. You perform them, sometimes well, other times with avoidance, and as such they are not always energising or connected to personal growth. Much focus can be made on employability and skills. This is a common rhetoric in higher education, especially in supporting students for graduation. However, there is little consensus on what skills are best that actually foster employability (Suleman, 2016). Let's have a look more closely at the difference between skills and strengths in Table 2.2.

Table 2.2 The differences between skills and strengths

Strengths	Skills
A natural disposition towards	Can be developed and learnt
Motivates you	Good at
Challenges you in a good way	Can do
Energises you	Energy changes
Talents	Satisfaction changes
Pushes you/always learning	Often the use of these skills drain you
Can work on (develop)	
Promote virtuous behaviour and wellbeing	Can get associated to these skills
Used often/opportunities arise	Not always so excited about them
Excites you	

In this book we focus on bringing our attention to both skills and strengths. They are both useful, but we like to think that a strengths-based approach is more conducive to collaboration.

What might this look like in practice? Let's connect with one of the authors. This is a nice example of how Narelle connected to her strength of creativity to support the formation of a collaboration. In this example, think about: How can we make time to use our strengths? To mindfully make the time and be present with the strengths so that we can enable ourselves to flourish in a collaboration, and well as to support others to flourish?

What could academic collaboration mean for me?

One of Narelle's strengths is creativity (this has been identified through VIA and also Strengths Profiler self-assessment tools). In her approach to writing, and learning and teaching, approach working with others through placing your strengths as a focus for your engagement. We will move between mindful reflective questions for you to work through and questions to consider connecting to the four case studies to support your growth in approaching collaborations.

Individual work within a team: Mindfulness and reflection

In terms of approaching collaborations, how can you utilise concepts of mindfulness to assist you to work with your strengths? As we discussed earlier in this chapter, mindfulness and being present and aware non-judgementally is a way that you can connect to your strengths. You may wish to link to your strengths through the free VIA strengths self-assessment tool as a way to provide you with a language or you can connect to your own self-observations to consider these mindful reflective questions. We call this strength spotting:

How can you be present with your strengths?

- What awareness arises for you when being curious about the strengths that energise you?
- What energises you and helps you in your approach to being an academic collaborator?
- What de-energises or makes you feel drained?
- What strength(s) could you identify that may be needed to be dialled down (used less) or paired with an energising strength that can support you to grow as an academic collaborator?

- What strengths do you admire in others? How could you learn more about these in action?
- How does what you do contribute to the team and how you feel about it?

Working collaboratively and building skills and strengths

Whether you are starting with a new collaboration or reflecting upon a collaboration that is already in the process of working together, the questions over the different stages of the Taxonomy of Collaboration support a reconnection to how you can work together and build your capacity to work with strengths (Figure 2.2). In this next section we invite you to think about how you approach or could approach a collaboration (noting we are inviting you to rethink and reconsider how you approach collaborations with strengths in mind). Table 2.3 offers some reflective questions as a starting point.

Individual responsibilities: Communicating, planning, organising, managing

When it comes to working with a collaboration it is important to be aware of how you work. Communication, planning, organisation, and managing your own way of working are imperative for success, not only for your contribution, but with others. Most often collaborations in higher education involve working across organisational and disciplinary boundaries. As such, these cross-cultural factors require us to acknowledge our own and others difference in how we see the world. Both disciplinary and interdisciplinary lenses can come into play, as well as

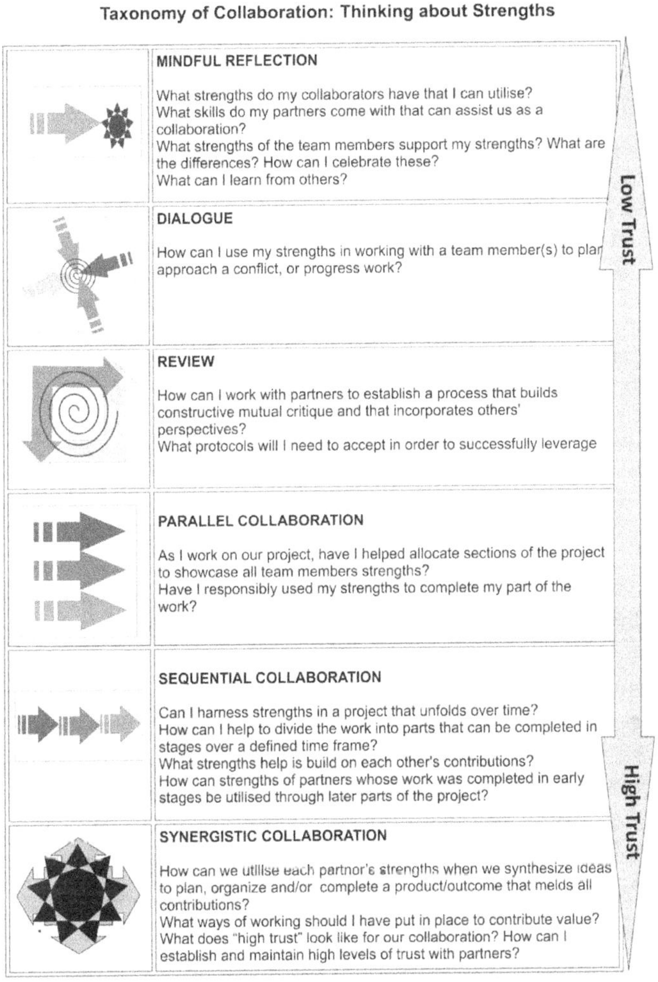

Collaboration skills and strengths 39

Taxonomy of Collaboration: Thinking about Strengths

	MINDFUL REFLECTION What strengths do my collaborators have that I can utilise? What skills do my partners come with that can assist us as a collaboration? What strengths of the team members support my strengths? What are the differences? How can I celebrate these? What can I learn from others?
	DIALOGUE How can I use my strengths in working with a team member(s) to plan approach a conflict, or progress work?
	REVIEW How can I work with partners to establish a process that builds constructive mutual critique and that incorporates others' perspectives? What protocols will I need to accept in order to successfully leverage
	PARALLEL COLLABORATION As I work on our project, have I helped allocate sections of the project to showcase all team members strengths? Have I responsibly used my strengths to complete my part of the work?
	SEQUENTIAL COLLABORATION Can I harness strengths in a project that unfolds over time? How can I help to divide the work into parts that can be completed in stages over a defined time frame? What strengths help is build on each other's contributions? How can strengths of partners whose work was completed in early stages be utilised through later parts of the project?
	SYNERGISTIC COLLABORATION How can we utilise each partner's strengths when we synthesize ideas to plan, organize and/or complete a product/outcome that melds all contributions? What ways of working should I have put in place to contribute value? What does "high trust" look like for our collaboration? How can I establish and maintain high levels of trust with partners?

(arrow from Low Trust at top to High Trust at bottom)

Figure 2.2 Working collaboratively and building skills and strengths.

Table 2.3 Mindfulness presence in supportive and unsupportive collaborations

Supportive collaborations	Unsupportive collaborations
Self-awareness	Lack of self-awareness
Curiosity	Incurious
Social connectivity	Social connectivity tensions
Harmonious interpersonal relationships	Volatile interpersonal relationships
Full engagement	Active work disengagement
Openness to others' perspectives	High levels of reactivity
	Rush to judgement
Non-judgemental space created	Expression of negative emotions
Self-regulation of emotions	Lack of self-reflection
Self-reflection	

varied communication styles and ways of approaching planning, organising, and managing teams. While we have opportunity to work with others and to learn about our self as well as how others approach these aspects, often our approaches are also influenced by our educational experiences and our ability to evaluate ourselves (Salmons, 2019). Although we come together usually driven by content or subject matter, there is opportunity to learn much about the collaborative process. This is where the Taxonomy of Collaboration allows us to reflect upon approaches.

Key questions to consider at the planning stage

- How will you approach the planning stage?
- What negotiations need to occur? What agreements are essential given the nature of the project and characteristics of the partners?

- How and when will you meet? When will you meet in person or use synchronous technologies?
- What are your communication protocols? What do these look like in action? How will you communicate asynchronously, with email, shared files, or text messages?
- How will you organise information and records be maintained? Will there be a shared storage source?
- How will you manage the team? Who leads? Who motivates?
- How do you know a task had been actioned?

Selecting an appropriate collaborative partner

In selecting an appropriate collaborative partner, it is important to think through the potential for advantage or inertia. Sometimes we rush into collaborations or we are placed into a team. In both these situations we need to frame the opportunity with curiosity, and avoid making snap judgements. This includes being self-aware, including awareness to the commitment we will make to the collaboration. From this mindset, participation is an act of kindness towards self, not something that we regret or that moves us to be hard on our self, or indeed others (Lemon, 2018). Consider these mindful reflective questions:

Key questions to consider at the partner selection stage

- If I am being asked to join a collaborative project, what is being asked of me? If I am inviting others, am I clearly communicating my expectations? If we are assigned to the project, how will we develop shared expectations?

- Do we have similar values and commitment to the project?
- Why do they want me to be a part of their team? What contribution can I make?
- Do we have a shared understanding of our strengths and potential contributions?
- How do I understand how others work? What skills and strengths do they possess and how do they complement mine?
- How will we approach time, working with others, respect of other work commitments, solving problems, and conflict?
- How can we learn from each other?
- How can I nurture others and build a good collaborative culture?

Individuals and the group: Degrees of autonomy

Autonomy 'promotes self-initiation and subjective ownership of work goals by acknowledging the perspective of workers, providing choice (where it exists) and rationales for requested tasks' (Spence, 2017, p. 123). Autonomy can support motivation in how one feels as a part of a collaboration in the workplace. Several studies have reported on the importance of need of supportive environments for autonomy and autonomous motivation to surface (Gillet, Gagné, Sauvagère, & Fouquereau, 2013; Hardre & Reeve, 2009; Schultz, Ryan, Niemiec, Legate, & Williams, 2014). Trépanier, Fernet, and Austin (2013) found that autonomous self-regulation for work activities that one is involved in and completing is associated with higher levels of transformational leadership. That is, the perception of autonomous self-regulation is one of being effective, able to inspire others, and simulate their interest.

As you work in collaborations in higher education it becomes evident that for autonomy to be valued there needs to be an establishment of non-controlling language, the provision of choice where possible, self-initiation encouragement, and, most importantly, the willingness to engage with, and genuinely acknowledge, other perspectives (Spence, 2017).

Through the integration of a mindful reflective stance, consideration can be made for what supportive and unsupportive collaborations can look like (refer to Table 2.3).

Key questions to address to form mutually supportive collaborations

- What boundaries do I need to establish to take care of myself? Of my partners? What boundaries need to be set for the collaboration to be to establish a supportive approach?
- What excites me? Who excites me? What ideas excite me? What gives me energy? What drains me of energy? How can I be self-aware of these energy levels and how they impact on my contribution to a supportive collaboration?
- What systems and agreements can be put in place to develop a supportive collaboration? Think about

language, inclusion, choice, engagement and formation of a mutual respect to support sharing of different perspectives.
- What systems and agreements can be put in place to develop systems and agreements for problem-solving and conflict resolution?

A successful collaboration requires a self-awareness of how you work under pressure. This is relevant to both problem-solving and conflict resolution. Hibbert and Huxham (2005) remind us that we are always learning in associated with understanding how to make judgements – about self and others as we manage to establish trust, create and meet goals, and see opportunity in collaborative contexts. Some of us find working with others easy, and some of us find it difficult. We come to collaborations with varied lived experiences. And when thinking about how we approach problem-solving and conflict resolution these lived experiences are crucial to be aware of, without judgement.

As you progress through various collaborative experiences, considering where you come from is important. At the beginning of a collaboration is the best time to establish how you can learn from one another in times of pressure. This is an ideal time as you are still beginning to learn about one another.

Key questions to help collaborative partners relate to each other in positive ways

- How can you translate your strengths in forming trust with your collaborators?
- What steps will you take to establish mutual respect?
- What protocols should be put in place proactively to support problem-solving?

- How agreements need to be put in place proactively to ensure successful conflict resolution?
- What will the best way be to communicate any issues that may arise?
- What steps will you take to deepen trusting relationships that allow for processing and moving through problems or conflicts?

Dynamics of a collaboration change over time. Ideally, they move towards the positive but, in reality, there can be times when a tension exists. As an individual you may witness this or perhaps be a part of the tension. Issues are more difficult to solve when expectations of working together become present. Often what can become present is a withdrawal or low engagement. Deci and Ryan (1985), in their work on self-determination theory, found that conflict can exist between one's natural orientation towards growth and development in interaction with disruptive experiences (such as peer pressure restriction, not feeling valued, lacking a sense of belonging, etc.). These disruptive experiences can impair, block or hinder autonomy and motivation, impacting upon overall success both individually and collaboratively. This is where utilising your strengths and the strengths of your collaborators can benefit a shifting of experience and understanding. Strengths can become a language to reconnect and support a positive approach (Green et al., 2017).

Take it away

In this chapter we invited you to pause and mindfully reflect upon how you approach collaborations from an individual perspective. In doing so we have invited you to consider your strengths and think about the strengths of how you might approach your partner. This is a part of taking a pause and being aware of the collaboration what you hope to achieve as part of the learning experience that is a collaboration. We acknowledge that this is not something we usually do, but disrupt usual practice to support the experience of success and growth. We encourage this as part of a formation of a spirit of curiosity and openness to what might be possible.

Try it! Exercises and questions for discussion or reflection

In other chapters we invite you to mindfully reflect about various different stages of a project and how you position yourself with collaborative partners. Throughout this chapter, we introduced you to the practice of thinking about your own strengths to frame your collaborations. Individuals who are a part of the collaborative process need to make sense of their own roles within a collaboration. No matter your situation we invite you to apply this thinking to new or existing situations. Moving forward, how will you try this? Consider how a strengths-based approach will look in your situation. Start by thinking through these questions:

- How will you identify and work with strengths and skills as an individual and with collaborative partners?
- How will focusing on strengths in the ways you discuss your project enhance your ability to reach collaborative advantage?

- Consider how you approach communication, organising and managing the team, problem-solving, and conflict resolution. What protocols do you need to put into place for the collaboration to be viewed as successful by partners and stakeholders?
- How will autonomy be honoured?
- How will mindful reflection be a part of your individual practice and the collective approach?
- How will you remain curious throughout the process of collaboration?

References

Biswas-Diener, R., Kashdan, T., & Lyubchik, N. (2017). Psychological strengths at work. In L. G. Oades, M. F. Steger, A. Delle Fave, & J. Passmore (Eds.), *The Wiley Blackwell handbook of the psychology of positivity and strengths-based approaches at work* (pp. 34–47). Chichester, UK: Wiley Blackwell.

Deci, E. L., & Ryan, R. M. (1985). *Intrinsic motivation and self-determination in human behavior*. New York: Plenum.

Dubreuil, P., Forest, J., & Courcy, F. (2014). From strengths use to work performance: The role of harmonious passion, subjective vitality and concentration. *The Journal of Positive Psychology*, 9(4), 335–349.

Dweck, C. S. (2017). *Mindset: Changing the way you think to fulfil your potential*. London: Robinson.

Gillet, N., Gagné, M., Sauvagère, S., & Fouquereau, E. (2013). The role of supervisor autonomy support, organizational support, and autonomous and controlled motivation in predicting employees' satisfaction and turnover intentions. *European Journal of Work and Organizational Psychology*, 22(4), 450–460.

Green, S., McQuaid, M., Purtell, A., & Dulagil, A. (2017). The psychology of positivity at work. In L. G. Oades, M. F. Steger, A. Delle Fave, & J. Passmore (Eds.), *The Wiley Blackwell handbook of the psychology of positivity and strengths-based approaches at work* (pp. 11–33). Chichester, UK: Wiley Blackwell.

Govindji, R., & Linley, P. A. (2007). Strengths use, self-concordance and well-being: Implications for strengths coaching and coaching psychologists. *International Coaching Psychology Review*, *2*, 143–153.

Hardre, P. L., & Reeve, J. (2009). Training corporate managers to adopt a more autonomy-supportive motivating style toward employees: An intervention study. *International Journal of Training and Development*, *13*(3), 165–184.

Hibbert, P., & Huxham, C. (2005). The carriage of tradition: Knowledge and its past in network contexts. *Management Learning*, *42*(1), 7–24.

Hodges, T. D., & Asplund, J. (2010). Strengths development in the workplace. In P. A. Linley, S. Harrington, & N. Garcea (Eds.), *Oxford handbook of positive psychology and work* (pp. 213–220). New York: Oxford University Press.

Kabat-Zinn, J. (1994). *Wherever you go, there you are: Mindfulness meditation in everyday life*. New York: Hyperion.

Lemon, N. (2018). I'm not playing the academic hunger games: Self-awareness and mindful practices in approaching research collaborations. In N. Lemon & S. McDonough (Eds.), *Mindfulness in the academy: Practices and perspectives from scholars* (pp. 129–154). Singapore: Springer.

Linley, A. (2008). *Average to A+: Realising strengths in yourself and others (strengthening the world series)*. Coventry, England: CAPP Press.

Linley, P. A., & Harrington, S. (2006). Playing to your strengths. *The Psychologist*, *19*, 86–89.

Lopez, S. J., Teramoto Pedrotti, J., & Snyder, C. R. (2015). *Positive psychology: The scientific and practical explorations of human strengths*. Thousand Oaks: SAGE.

Louis, M. C., & Lopez, S. J. (2014). Strengths interventions: Current progress and future directions. In A. C. Parks & S. M. Schueller (Eds.), *The Wiley Blackwell handbook of positive psychological interventions* (pp. 66–89). Chichester, UK: John Wiley & Sons, Ltd.

McGovern, T. V., & Miller, S. L. (2008). Integrating teacher behaviors with character strengths and virtues for faculty development. *Teaching of Psychology*, *35*, 278–285.

McQuaid, M., & Lawn, E. (2014). *Your strengths blueprint: How to be engaged, energized, and happy at work*. Albert Park, VA: Michelle McQuaid Pty Ltd.

Niemiec, R. M. (2014). *Mindfulness and character strengths: A practical guide to flourishing*. Boston, MA: Hogrefe Publishing.

Niemiec, R. M., Rashid, T., & Spinella, M. (2012). Strong mindfulness: Integrating mindfulness and character strengths. *Journal of Mental Health Counseling*, *34*(3), 240–253.

Oades, L. G., Steger, M. F., Delle Fave, A., & Passmore, J. (2017). *The Wiley Blackwell handbook of the psychology of positivity and strengths-based approaches at work*. Chichester, UK: Wiley Blackwell.

Peterson, C., & Seligman, M. E. P. (2004). *Character strengths and virtues: A handbook and classification*. Washington, DC: American Psychological Association.

Peterson, C., Stephens, J. P., Park, N., Lee, F., & Seligman, M. E. P. (2009). Strengths of character and work. In P. A. Linley, S. Harrington, & N. Garcea (Eds.), *Oxford handbook of positive psychology and work* (pp. 221–234). Oxford, UK: Oxford University Press.

Roffey, S. (2017). Positive relationships at work. In L. G. Oades, M. F. Steger, A. Delle Fave, & J. Passmore (Eds.), *The Wiley Blackwell handbook of the psychology of positivity and strengths-based approaches at work* (pp. 171–190). Chichester, UK: Wiley Blackwell.

Salmons, J. (2019). *Learning to collaborate, collaborating to learn*. Sterling, VA: Stylus Publishing, LLC.

Schultz, P. P., Ryan, R. M., Niemiec, C. P., Legate, N., & Williams, G. C. (2014). Mindfulness, work climate, and psychological need satisfaction in employee well-being. *Mindfulness*, *6*(5), 971–985.

Spence, G. B. (2017). Mindfulness at work. In L. G. Oades, M. F. Steger, A. Delle Fave, & J. Passmore (Eds.), *The Wiley Blackwell handbook of the psychology of positivity and strengths-based approaches at work* (pp. 100–131). Chichester, UK: Wiley Blackwell.

Suleman, F. (2016). Employability skills of higher education graduates: Little consensus on a much-discussed subject. *Procedia – Social and Behavioral Sciences*, *228*(2016), 169–174.

Trépanier, S.-G., Fernet, C., & Austin, S. (2013). The moderating role of autonomous motivation in the job demands–strain relation: A two sample study. *Motivation and Emotion*, *37*, 93–105.

VIA Institute on Character. (2018). VIA character survey. Retrieved from http://www.viacharacter.org/www/Character-Strengths-Survey

Waters, L. (2017). *The strength switch*. North Sydney, NSW: Penguin Random House Australia.

Wood, A. M., Linley, P. A., Maltby, J., Kashdan, T. B., & Hurling, R. (2011). Using personal and psychological strengths leads to increases in well-being over time: A longitudinal study and the development of the strengths use questionnaire. *Personality and Individual Differences*, *50*(1), 15–19.

3 Collaboration and the PhD experience

What will you learn by studying this chapter?

This chapter focuses on the collaboration between doctoral student and supervisor, characterising their relationship as being centred around collaboration. The chapter outlines the place of self-care in this process, connecting to one's why of undertaking doctoral studies, acknowledging the place of vision and values and how they can be different for each individual, and the role of social support and how this can be achieved through different mechanisms within and outside of the academy. Mindful strategies focusing on awareness and being curious are shared to support the unpacking of case studies and to make connections between them.

In this chapter you will gain an understanding of:

- Self-care and its importance to you.
- Connecting to your why and job crafting.
- Wellbeing in association with your approach to being a doctoral student.
- Relationships and how seeking out others can support you.
- What collaborating up and across can look like.

The big picture: Self-care is not a dirty word

Self-care is anything you can do to help your physical, mental or emotional health – it's about our capacity to choose behaviours that allows you to balance stressors (Richards, Sheen & Mazzer, 2014). Self-care is a proactive action (Reading, 2018) that focuses on steps to develop, protect, maintain and improve health, wellbeing or wellness (Self Care Forum, 2019). There are a variety of, and indeed combination of approaches and strategies you can engage with to help you with this (Figure 3.1). Discussions around self-care have become more prevalent in recent times as many of us are feeling pressure in life; in that we are always connected, juggling multiple demands, feeling time-poor, managing multiple roles across different areas of our lives, and feeling the load of

Figure 3.1 Self-care is worthy of our attention.

assumptions and expectations that we put on our self personally and professionally.

It is important to remind ourselves of the act of self-care. Self-care allows us to be and become our best for ourselves and our collaborative partners. Taking care of ourselves is part of being responsible to others.

Undertaking a PhD is a lengthy process and taking care of yourself is an imperative to last the distance. Your PhD study is a long process with many key milestones that are exciting but also mentally, emotionally, and physically draining). And we acknowledge that 'self-care has been somewhat neglected in higher education institutions' (Walton, Aquino, Talbot & Melia, 2019, p. 123).

At the core of self-care is an awareness that placing self first in terms of caring for yourself mentally, emotionally, and physically is not selfish. It is important to do, as if you do not look after your own wellbeing, you will find that you are unable to sufficiently care for others or even your work. Looking after yourself does not mean ignoring others; rather, it should embrace connection with others (Neff, 2011). It is not a dirty word, but a way to focus on how you can look after yourself in order to be the best version of you. Tuning into what you need and asking the question of 'What do I need right now?' is a great starting point to explore your self-care needs. This approach is not selfish, rather it allows you to position yourself in a way that means you are being true to you.

The *Five Ways to Wellbeing* designed by the New Economics Foundation (NEF, 2010) reminds us that we need to be well rounded in order to support our wellbeing. They note the five areas of:

1. Connect
2. Be active

3. Take notice
4. Give
5. Keep learning

This framework provides you with a great way to consider self-care from a mindful perspective, drawing, in particular, on notions of awareness and curiosity. Under each of these areas we invite you to think about how you show your self-care, and to take time to map this in the table provided (Table 3.1). We recommend that you do this often to remind yourself of the importance to be well rounded in your wellbeing, especially at pressure points associated with being a doctoral student.

In your mapping, what do you notice? Are there moments that show good patterns of behaviour? Perhaps there are some gaps?

In considering your self-care routines in this holistic manner, moving forward will require you to engage with those practices and behaviours that support you, while at the same time recognising you have some gaps that may

Table 3.1 Mapping our self-care routines

Five ways to wellbeing	*List your self-care routines or strategies*
Connect – how do you connect with others?	
Be active – what do you do to move your body?	
Take notice – how are you curious?	
Give – what do you do for others?	
Keep learning – what is something new you have been spending time on?	

impede you or that may benefit from some particular attention (especially when you are feeling under pressure). Walton et al. (2019) offer some advice for thinking about the application of self-care, and we have pulled together some of their best top tips, including:

- Celebrate milestones by engaging in some well-deserved self-care – you've earned it! (p. 47).
- Schedule in time for self-care activities into your daily/weekly routine (p. 68).
- Think 3 Ps – Planning; Prioritising; and Playing – and how these fit into one day (p. 118).
- Consider planning in self-care days, just as you would for medical and other health appointments (p. 118).
- Accept setbacks as part of the journey (p. 125).
- Don't be afraid to ask for help (p. 125).
- Learn to be patient (p. 126).
- Build both work and non-work networks (p. 126).
- Do not compare yourself with others (p. 126).
- Know what makes you happy (p. 126).
- Sleep well (p. 126).
- Exercise and eat well (p. 126).
- The importance of weekends (p. 126).
- Take a break and travel (p. 126).

When more than self-care is needed

We also want to acknowledge that some situations cannot be resolved through self-care or drawing upon social support (such as your peers, supervisors and/or network). Self-care is a starting point for you to think about habits and routines that support you. Sometimes our mental and emotional wellbeing needs extra nurturing and we highly recommend seeking professional support (seeing a social worker, counsellor or psychologist). It is also important to note that you may require time away from your studies (a decision you can make in partnership with your supervisors or academic team).

In Chapter 4 we will connect your wellbeing and collaboration with the PERMAH framework – Positive emotions, engagement, relationships, meaning, accomplishment, and health. This is a way to connect you to your overall wellbeing while thinking about your strengths and skills individually and collectively. It is one way, another way, to approach looking after you. As you begin to think about extending your self-care routines, you may also wish to connect with this framework. It is another suggestion for you, one that may or may not resonate with your individual needs. Here are some questions to consider:

- How could these pillars (positive emotions, engagement, relationships, meaning, accomplishments, and health) support your approach to self-care?
- How can you seek advice from your supervisor?
- How could you work with your supervisor to support self-care routines?
- How could you enact these aspects of self-care in approaching a collaboration with your supervisor?

Connecting to your why: Purpose, career aspirations, impact, and satisfaction

Connecting to your *why* is an important first step to working out *how* to achieve the goals that excite you. Your why is connected to your self-care, how you care for yourself and indeed how you care for others with your contribution(s), and it is a large part of creating a life you enjoy living (versus merely surviving!). As doctoral students connecting to your why is often associated to your work – your PhD, how you came to undertake a PhD, and what impact you would like to have. But your why is not only about your work. It is as much about your meaning, your passions, and what drives you holistically.

In connecting to your why you will often find that the nature of what you are doing, your passion for the work you do and what contribution you want to make are all significant elements of your why. It is the bigger picture of why you are doing what you are doing. We can also find that there are some activities, collaborations, or experiences that take us away from this why or blur it (this can be a time when tensions can emerge for us) as much as inspire it (when we feel highly motivated and engaged).

Self-care and job crafting

Let's connect self-care and your why with the concept of job crafting. This is where we can reshape our job (in this case carrying out the PhD and what it is connected to (your work in higher education or in industry or where you are heading) in such a way that what we do becomes more closely aligned with your why – motivations, as well as your individual strengths, skills and preferences. Job crafting is a process that allows you to reshape and rethink about the nature of the job itself, including the demands experienced on the PhD as well as a personal sense of efficacy for meeting those demands (Slemp, Kern & Vella-Brodrick, 2015). Wellbeing in the workplace correlates with employee punctuality and time efficiency, less absenteeism, higher retention (Spector 1997), increased productivity, profit (Harter et al. 2002) in work-related outcomes over an extended period of time. Workplace wellbeing is linked the desirable outcomes such as job retention and enhanced performance (Harter et al. 2002; Warr 1999).

It helps us if we can reshape and craft what it is we do, and, more importantly, how we approach it. And collaboration is a part of this. Job crafting is connected significantly to working to our strengths and seeing opportunity to perhaps at times rethink how we approach a task or aspect of the job. This requires an alignment between your knowledge, strengths, skills, needs, and preferences and the demands and requirements of the job (Edwards, 1991; Slemp, 2017). When alignment is in place you can become fully engaged and satisfied because you are sufficiently challenged without feeling overwhelmed (Warr & Inceoglu, 2012). This is where the work you have done in Chapter 2, and will do in Chapter 4, with your strengths begins to be put in practice. We'll connect with some strategies for this later in this chapter – in the meantime, however, how could you craft your PhD experience to connect to your why? How could you craft your supervisory relationship to support your why?

As doctoral students, and indeed with all our work, we are increasingly seeking to derive meaning, happiness, and social connections from our work, as well as opportunities for professional learning and personal growth (Avolio & Sosik 1999). Recent research highlights the shift towards employees taking a more active role in shaping their tasks, their environment, and their overall experiences in the workplace (Slemp, 2017). For you as doctoral students this is empowering. It enables you to think about your why and what you would like to achieve. For working in collaboration with your supervisor(s), this enables a way think about, or craft how you can approach your studies, research, and future plans.

We can connect with our why by thinking about workplace wellbeing and taking a proactive approach from both hedonic (affect, satisfaction, etc.) and eudaimonic (meaning, engagement, etc.) experiences (Page & Vella-Brodrick, 2009). Having a greater understanding of the factors that influence your wellbeing (and including your self-care routines) can help you to have greater control over your work/PhD experiences to increase wellbeing, satisfaction, and experiences associated to working in higher education.

Collaborating up, across and passing it on

Relationships are key to our wellbeing. As we noted in Chapter 2, they are fundamental for connecting to meaning and offer much in the way of support. They are also crucial to our self-care routines and our why. As a doctoral student you will experience many levels of relationships that come with collaboration – for example, supervision, committees, peers, industry partnerships, etc. In higher education relationships are key, often connected to mentoring (official or unofficial) and in ways that are between individuals across different academic levels. Thus, creating opportunities for connection that scaffold our personal and professional growth. In this way relationships can scaffold our learning and growth through (Ambler, Harvey & Cahir, 2016):

- Supporting personal development and professional enhancement;
- Improving research, professional learning, and/or teaching;
- Engaging in self-reflection; and
- Encouraging new ways of thinking.

How this can look for each of us can be different. By connecting to our discipline, skills development, strengths, and emotional needs, we can identify who we may connect with to support our learning and growth professionally. Table 3.2 offers some triggers to think about this in how you could approach your relationships and what they can offer you, with an awareness that not one person can do all of these things (i.e. one supervisor); rather, you can put together a collection of people to assist you (i.e., supervision team, postdoctoral team, peers, others in your field).

Let's have a look at some common collaborations as a doctoral student and the way the relationship can be crafted.

Collaborating up

It would not be uncommon for most of you, as doctoral and early career researchers, to experience mentorship from your thesis supervisor(s). It is often our first connection point to mentoring in higher education. Some of us

Table 3.2 Approaches to relationship support and needs

Discipline	Skills development	Emotional
How can working with others help you to:	How can working with others help you to develop:	How can working with others help you to create a space to seek:
Understand how your discipline has evolved. Recognise and explore your questions. Identify innovative ways of engaging with collaborations, research ideas, or work through teaching problems. Understand your discipline, its focuses, questions, and/or methodologies in relation to other fields. Make connections outside of academia. Translate impact to desired audiences.	Communication skills across a variety of formats for different audiences. Collaboration skills. Leadership skills. Learning and teaching pedagogies. Research trajectory. Working with industry. Develop partnerships. Planning skills. Time management skills. Approaches to different writing genres.	Perspective. Advice. Support for rephrasing, refocusing or processing, etc. Emotional support. Explore your lived experiences. Connection with others Safe/honest supportive dialogue. Exploration of your why. Exploration of your self-care routines. Extension and growth of your self-care routines.

expect mentoring and others do not. We acknowledge this can look different for everyone, and may indeed not be present for some of you, but more commonly than not the first experience of co-writing or co-researching is with your supervision team. This is a relationship we frame as collaborating up. This is also where you need to be able to acknowledge you are in a power relationship and as such there can be some awkward moments, especially if things go pear-shaped. But they don't have to be like this. Some of the most significant developments in relationships and mentorships can come from the navigation and mutual respect underpinned by being open and establishing protocols. When approached with an awareness, openness and curiosity, what can seem a moment of tension can build a way of working and a solid relationship. This time of your professional academic development is also significant as it can set you up for good practices, and ability to produce to meet your key milestones, but also contribute to the research community and your disciplines or portfolio of work. Collaborating up requires you to consciously plan for, engage in, and be active while embracing learning from those who are more experienced. Think about:

- How do you want to work with your supervisor for guidance on professional enhancement?
- What can you learn from collaborating up?
- What protocols might you need to negotiate and put in place?
- What are your intentions when you meet with your supervisor?

As you move through doctoral stage to early career researcher or if you are working in both spaces (as an early career research in an institution while completing your studies or as a postdoc for example), you will also find you will be collaborating up in learning and teaching situations, research groups, and/or committees. Once more you can find some of these experiences motivating and sometimes deflating. All these situations offer an opportunity to learn. To learn how your skills and strengths can contribute to the partnership, and also learn how you want to be, much aligned to the idea of *Circle of Niceness* introduced in the following chapter (Chapter 4). We frame collaborating up as a way to experience mentoring. It can be official (the individual knows) or not (you learn from them through observation and experience). As such, this opportunity creates opportunities for personal development and professional enhancement; improvement; engaging in self-reflection; new ways of thinking; building professional relationships; supporting personal development and professional enhancement; improving teaching, professional learning, and research; engaging in self-reflection; and encouragement of new ways of thinking (Ambler, Harvey & Cahir, 2016).

Collaborating across

Undertaking doctoral study can be one of the most challenging, stressful, and isolating experiences of an academic career (Cumerma, 2018; Walton et al., 2019). Connecting with others will be one of the most significant self-care routines you can undertake. We acknowledge that connecting with your peers will be a huge part of this.

As a doctoral student collaborating across means seeking out social support with your peers. It is heavily based in forming a network. This can come in many forms, for example, in shared offices, at institutional or national conferences, with writing groups (e.g.: face-to-face within your institution or across or virtually (e.g.: #ACWRI or Academic Writing Month also known as #*AcWriMo*) or #PhDchat on Twitter or Shut Up and Write groups), support groups, online groups (e.g.: Women in Academia Support Network or *Doctorate Support* Group on Facebook), writing retreats, or through doctoral research support. Core to these approaches is reaching out and forming relationships with those who are also at similar stages in their career to you and who can understand the complexity of being a doctoral student.

So how might you approach this? Let's connect with Walton et al. (2019) 'Three Cs' of postgraduate study (pp. 129–134) in Table 3.3.

Collaborating across means that you are able to seek support but also offer support – we call this passing it on, that is to share what you have been learning in approaches to writing, managing time, working with your supervisor orcompleting milestones of the doctoral journey. In collaborating across with openness and curiosity you are beginning to be a part of the *Circle of Niceness* – where sharing, reciprocity, mutual respect, and celebrating learning moments for yourself and others can be enacted. We will unpack this further in Chapter 4. Key to collaborating across is learning from one another.

- How can you utilise your peers for support?
- How can you be proactive in creating opportunities?
- How might you extend your networks to support you in the doctoral journey?

Table 3.3 'Three Cs' of postgraduate study

Three Cs	Description
Capability	Take a realistic assessment of your current skill set. Identify areas for growth, and address them. Celebrate your achievements.
Consistency	Treat your postgraduate studies like a 'regular' job. If you work 'overtime' one day, take it off 'in lieu' later. Try to establish a routine. Remember to take time to reflect.
Communication	Turn to your supervisor(s). Utilise your wider social circle. Engage with the wider postgraduate community. Consider how you can work on campus and off campus, or connect in virtually to opportunities if you are remote. Consider how social media may support you (blogging, tweeting, hashtag-focused discussions, Facebook groups, being an observer or active participant). Attend postgraduate sessions and events at conferences. Utilise institutional postgraduate conferences. Attend PhD-focused sessions and visiting scholar lecturers to connect with others.

Cases and examples

Let's work with two of our case studies, Phillipe and Alicia.

Phillipe is excited about the opportunity to work with someone else on writing a paper for a peer-reviewed journal. He has experienced a positive way of working and is confident to use the model he has experienced with this new author, although he is beginning to see some signs of imposter syndrome as he navigates this new co-writing partnership. As Phillipe works with a fellow PhD peer, he realises that his peer is unfamiliar with the model he used with his supervisors to write his first journal paper. As they meet discussions about how to approach and what to do are moving fast. Too fast for him to understand at times and see how the approach is a collaboration. At the moment, the plan is to write independently. It doesn't feel like a collaboration for Phillipe. A deadline has been set and when he considers this, this is overwhelming as he is simultaneously working towards a conference presentation and a PhD milestone of a mid-candidature panel review. After the last meeting with co-writer, he felt totally lost.

Phillipe regroups and decides that he needs to let his co-writer know, even though this feels as if he is showing a weakness. As he ponders more, gives space, seeks advice about the approach, and thinks about his past writing experiences with his supervisors, Phillipe realises he can support a model for negotiation of a different approach that feels more inclusive and organic. He also connects with his skill set of being able to plan while also drawing on the strengths of curiosity and perseverance. Phillipe knows he needs to collaborate across. With awareness and setting the intention to be able to communicate his needs he is able to connect back to his why and also his self-care routines – working to a fast-paced timeline is exciting and motivating but when there is confusion in allocation, approach, and realistic time frames. By stepping back he is able to ask the questions in the next meeting that support a conversation about timelines, allocation of writing sections, and how to move forward while learning from each other.

Alicia has attended a meeting with her supervision team, peers, and all stakeholders. She's confused about something that occurred in the meeting. Her supervisor seems to have nominated her to complete a significant task for one of the key stakeholders which doesn't align to original scoping of her work and timelines. And she is feeling that this task is taking her away from her focus. Alicia is feeling stressed. She is ruminating – thoughts are going around in her head that she feels like she has been misrepresented by her supervisor. She's worried this is going to be a future pattern, and Alicia can't stop wondering whether or not this postdoc team is right for her. There are tensions around a number of aspects: where she wants to be, who else she would be working with, thinking she has wasted her time, and 'what if?' scenarios, ranging from quitting, what will others think, what if I can't do it, and so on.

This is a wonderful example of where collaborating up is required. Alicia will benefit from thinking about the question 'What do you want your supervisor to know?'

After time away and speaking with her peers, Alicia is able to realise that ruminating is unhelpful, and that having a conversation with her supervisor is the most beneficial step. This conversation is tricky, however, as emotions are raw. With awareness, and being present with these emotions Alicia can put together a plan and create intentions for how she would like to approach the meeting. Her meeting agenda includes: (1) Connect to highlights of the meeting with the stakeholders (start with a positive); (2) Where to next with task allocation (connecting with the intention to seek clarification allowing opportunity to tune into what is required and how to align with other tasks); (3) Timelines (negotiating how this will look); and (4) Support approaches (connecting to support that can be accessed). At no stage during this meeting would she blame; rather, she should use 'I-messages' and ask clarifying questions to support a negotiation and inquiry underpinned by mutual respect and developing a professional working relationship with her supervisors at this time.

Into practice

In this next section we outline some strategies you can undertake to assist you to think about the PhD experience based on the concepts we have discussed in this chapter.

Have you connected to your why?

Here are some reflective questions to connect you to your why.

- What is your background? How did you come to be where you are right now?
- What are you interested in?
- What are your goals?
- What are your strengths?
- What skills and expertise do you bring?
- What impact do you want to make?
- What are you curious about?
- What do you want to be known for?
- What energises you?

In connecting further with your why it is important to connect with what energises you. Building from your reflections from the previous activity let's connect with the Japanese concept of *Ikigai,* or the reason for being. *Ikigai* is seen as the convergence of four primary elements:

- PASSION – What are you passionate about? What do you love?
- MISSION/IMPACT – What does the world need?
- VOCATION – What are you good at?
- PROFESSION – What you can get paid for? Now? In the future?

Thinking about *Ikigai:* How would you describe each of these areas in relation to your why and the why of you carrying out your doctoral studies? How do you build on your strengths? How can your self-care routines support you to connect in these ways and achieve your why? How can your self-care routines support you to be energised or return to your energy to help you achieve?

Mentorship

As we approach our doctoral studies the mentorship from our supervisor and others offers opportunity to be able to seek advice and to support our learning. With an awareness, openness, and curiosity, learning from others supports our seeking social support and connection. This is where relationships become crucial to what it is we want to achieve. Consider these questions in relation to thinking about how you can collaborate up and across:

- What does the relationship mean to you?
- Thinking about what the mentor offers and what you offer, how can you view this as a collaboration?
- What do you want to achieve?
- Is this relationship official or unofficial? What does this look like for you?
- How can you be open to this relationship changing or developing?
- Who is right for me right now?
- Who might I connect with in the future? What can they offer me? What would I like to ask them?

Solving problems: When you get stuck

Sometimes we can get stuck with our why and how we look after our self and show self-care. With this negotiation in yourself you also need to think about how you approach your collaboration with your supervisor and others. Sheldon, Jose, Kashdan, and Jarden (2015) remind us of ten key character strengths associated with achieving goals and wellbeing. We invite you to think about these in conjunction with your strengths, why and self-care as well as your relationships for collaboration.

1. Curiosity.
2. The sense of control over good and bad events.
3. Meaning in life.
4. Grit (perseverance).
5. Gratitude.
6. Use of strengths and knowledge.
7. Orientation towards happiness: Pleasure.
8. Orientation towards happiness: Engagement.
9. Orientation towards happiness: Meaning.
10. Savouring.

What do these look like for you when you get stuck? How can these ten key character strengths assist you to reframe? What patterns do you show in your routine when you are stressed verses being in flow?

Try it! Exercises and questions for discussion or reflection

Nurturing your collaboration with your supervisor

There are moments during the collaboration up phase with your supervisor that you need to consciously nurture this relationship a little more than usual. In collaborating up at moments where there may be tension or you need to problem-solve, how might you utilise these questions to support your approach? Think about these questions from a space of curiosity and awareness.

- What do you want your supervisor to know?
- How do you want to work with your supervisor(s)?
- Who else can advise you?
- Is your supervisor your mentor? Or is it a team approach? Is there someone else who might offer another perspective at this time? Are there multiple reference points for you at this time?
- What does problem-solving look like for you right now?
- What's your plan for right now?

Take it away

Collaboration and the doctoral experience is multi-layered. You are required to collaborate up and across. And this does look different to everyone. What we invite you to think about is how you can connect to learning from one another and connecting to concepts of self-care, your why, job crafting, and wellbeing while placing relationships at the heart of what you do. Key to your experience will be your relationship with your supervisor, and your peers. These are different versions of social support, but ones that offer different but complementary self-care support.

References

Ambler, T., Harvey, M., & Cahir, J. (2016). University academics' experiences of learning through mentoring. *Australian Educational Researcher*, *43*(5), 609–627.

Avolio, B. J., & Sosik, J. J. (1999). A life-span framework for assessing the impact of work on white-collar workers. In S. L. Willis & J. D. Reid (Eds.), *Life in the middle: psychological and social development in middle age* (pp. 251–274). San Diego: Academic Press.

Cumerma, A. (2018, 20 January). Smart people problems: We need to talk about PhD mental health. Times Higher Education. Retrieved from https://www.timeshighereducation.com/blog/smart-people-problems-we-need-talk-aboutphd-mental-health

Edwards, J. R. (1991). Person-job fit: a conceptual integration, literature review and methodological critique. *International Review of Industrial/ Organizational Psychology*, 6, 283–351.

Harter, J. K., Schmidt, F. L., & Hayes, T. L. (2002). Business-unit-level relationship between employee satisfaction, employee engagement, and business outcomes: a meta-analysis. *Journal of Applied Psychology*, 87, 268–279.

Harter, J. K., Schmidt, F. L., & Keyes, C. L. (2002). Well-being in the workplace and its relationship to business outcomes: A review of the Gallup studies. In C. L. Keyes & J. Haidt (Eds.), *Flourishing: the positive person and the good life* (pp. 205–224). Washington, D.C.: American Psychological Association.

Neff, K. (2011). *Self-compassion: stop beating yourself up and leave insecurity behind*. London: Harper Collins.

New Economics Foundation (NEF). (2010). Mental Capital and Wellbeing Project. Retrieved from https://issuu.com/neweconomicsfoundation/docs/five_ways_to_well-being?viewMode=presentation

Page, K. M., & Vella-Brodrick, D. A. (2009). The what, why and how of employee well-being: A new model. *Social Indicators Research*, 90, 441–458.

Reading, S. (2018). *The self-care revolution: Smart habits & simple practices to allow you to flourish*. Karol Bagh, Delhi: Aster.

Richards, K., Sheen, E., & Mazzer, M. C. (2014). *Self-care and you: Caring for the caregiver*. Silver Spring, MD: American Nurses Association.

Self-Care Forum. (2019). Self-Care Forum: Home. Retrieved July 27, 2019, from http://www.selfcareforum.org/

Sheldon, K. M., Jose, P. E., Kashdan, T. B. & Jarden, A. (2015). Personality, effective goal-striving, and enhanced well-being: Comparing 10 candidate personality strengths. *Personality and Social Psychology Bulletin*, 41(4), 575–585.

Slemp, G. R. (2017). Job Crafting. In L. G. Oades, M. F. Steger, A. Delle Fave, & J. Passmore (Eds.), *The Wiley Blackwell handbook of the psychology of positivity and strengths-based approaches at work* (pp. 342–365). West Sussex, UK: John Wiley & Sons, Ltd.

Slemp, G. R., Kern, M. L., & Vella-Brodrick, D. (2015). What is well-being the role of job crafting and coming support. *Psychology of Well-Being*, *5*(7), 1–7.

Spector, P. (1997). *Job satisfaction: application, assessment, causes and consequences*. California: Sage.

Walton, H., Aquino, M. R. J., Talbot, C. V., & Melia, C. (2019). *A guide for psychology postgraduates: Surviving postgraduate study* (2nd ed.). London: The British Psychological Society.

Warr, P. (1999). Well-being and the workplace. In D. Kahneman, E. Diener, & N. Schwarz (Eds.), *Well-being: the foundations of hedonic psychology* (pp. 392–412). New York: Russell Sage.

Warr, P., & Inceoglu, I. (2012). Job engagement, job satisfaction, and contrasting associations with person-job fit. *Journal of Occupational Health Psychology*, *17*, 129–138.

4 Collaboration skills and strengths
Working as a group

What will you learn by studying this chapter?

In this chapter we address skills and strengths in association to the collective perspective, building on the work we did in Chapter 2 looking at your approach to individual strengths and skills. We focus now on different reactions to working collaboratively, as for some working in a collaboration is not an organically straightforward process. We also look at how we can (re)frame our interactions around a concept called *Circle of Niceness*, underpinned by mutual respect and engagement in actions that support an embodiment way of being. We offer some strategies and illustrate them in the context of the exemplary cases.

In this chapter you will gain an understanding of:

- Skills and strengths associated to working with others.
- Ways of knowing yourself and being able to work with others.

- Ideas for how to develop skills and strengths as a collective.
- Approaching collaborations from a bigger context of spreading good academic behaviour.
- Problem-solving and conflict resolution as a group.

The big picture: From individual to group work

There is no surprise that working with our strengths and skills requires some self-reflection. When we think about our strengths we are being encouraged to connect with our natural predispositions, whereas when considering our skills, we are identifying something that can be developed and learnt. In Chapter 2 you started to look at yourself in relation to this way of thinking. In this chapter we focus on working with others and how to realise strengths in yourself and others to achieve better performance, satisfaction, and fulfilment. Firstly, let us consider some common collaborative practices, to begin to identify how strengths and skills can be matched together. This is not an exhaustive list, but more a connection point for you. We'll unpack these further as the chapter progresses.

Honesty as a **strength** might see you as a straightforward person, not only by speaking the truth but also by living your life in a genuine and authentic way.

By contrast, a **skill** related to this might be an ability to frame how you can be authentic with others by knowing how to select your words when under pressure or feeling stressed, or be able to step back and reflect before responding, or be able to take notes in order to be able to talk back to a situation.

Perseverance as a strength might see you as someone who does not get distracted when you work and you are able to get the work done on time (or even before the deadline), with a sense of satisfaction in completing your tasks.

By contrast, a **skill** related to this might be an ability to identify steps and chunk your time to complete these, organise a diary to assist partners to manage their deadlines for a project, or be able to successfully manage your time across multiple projects.

As we think about how we connect with our strengths and skills let's connect with Janet and an example of how she does this in practise. Janet relies on commitments to honesty and to perseverance when collaborating with others, and aims to live them. Honesty between partners also means we practice academic honesty and respect others' intellectual property. It means that we are open about what we can and cannot contribute to any collaboration. Honest partners bring questions or problems to the forefront, and don't talk badly about each other in private.

Perseverance means we are committed to the project. It is an essential quality to collaborations that involve more than a one-time experience. In long-term projects inertia, distractions, and emergencies will inevitably emerge, but partners who persevere don't allow the project to be derailed. Everyone is busy and any partner will have other work and personal priorities, but we need to know that we share a commitment both to the project and to each other. Janet believes flexibility and empathy are linked to perseverance. A missed deadline or incomplete draft is to be expected when partners are under pressure. One year, for example, Janet's house flooded; another year, two members of her immediate family were in end-of-life stages. If she was slow on a deliverable, she needed partners to understand that she was not reneging on her part of the project. Commitment to our partners must include the realisation that there are times when we simply have to bend a little and give each other space.

These two strengths are tied directly to trust. Can I trust that you will give this project your best effort? That you will honour our agreements, and communicate any disruptions? Can I trust that you are being honest with me about your contributions, and that what you write is your own work? Can I trust that you will be there for all stages of the project, especially the boring parts? A strengths-based approach means we are optimistic, but realistic when working with collaborative partners.

How do I and we develop mindfulness as a collective?

In Chapter 2 we talked about mindfulness and strengths and how to approach these with awareness, openness, curiosity and from a non-judgemental state where we can support self-improvement. In adopting such an approach we are always looking to grow, to put our best foot forward and to learn more about our self and others. So, what does this mean collectively?

Working to strengths and skills collectively is a lot about awareness and attention. Paying attention to self and others, being present (which can be a challenge in higher education as we are often juggling lots of different tasks at multiple times). Mindfulness offers us a way to connect with who we are.

Mindfulness tips for working with partners

Here are some points for you to consider when trying to develop mindful working with partners:

- **Identify and concentrate on your strengths.** By knowing you, you can begin to connect with others.
- **Name the strengths out loud.** Use the language of strengths, but be careful to not assume everyone knows their own strengths or what they look like in practice. Share your experience, share what you notice, or suggest an assessment tool to support next steps of discovery. This is often called strength spotting.
- **Give yourself permission to explore and develop your strengths.** Tune into what energises you.
- **Strength spot.** Notice others' strengths. Appreciate. Express gratitude.
- **Be careful not to compare with others.** We can identify with strengths in different ways and show them in different ways, so be careful not to compare, rather talk about what you notice (from 'I message' space).
- **When working with others, assign tasks based on an individual's strengths.** Look for ways to utilise each other's strengths. In order to be able to approach the task. You will need to have a conversation about this. What do they look like? How can they support individual and group cohesion? What does success look like?

- **Responsibility and accountability.** Think about how each of you can and will approach the task collectively. What are individual AND collective responsibilities? What are individual AND collective accountabilities? What does this look, feel, and sound like?
- **Motivate and celebrate.** How can you support and motivate one another?
- **Use failure as motivation.** Learning from mistakes is one way we can embody a growth mindset. How will you approach this individually and collectively? What might be a safe space or phrase that you can utilise to support the conversations? How can strengths support these conversations?
- **Create a habit.** Create a habit of using your strengths individually and collectively. What are patterns or routines you can put in place to support the honing of your and others' strengths on a regular basis that helps you and your partners to feel more engaged and energised?
- **Reflect.** Practise awareness and bringing your attention framing to your work with others.

Organisational culture and collaboration

Culture has been identified as one of the most powerful and stable forces in operation within an organisation (Howard, 1998; Schein, 1990). Each workplace, so in this case higher education institutions, is unique and is significantly influenced by survival (internal and external influences) (Howard, 1998). Varying environments influence wellbeing, including the workplace.

The workplace is an environment in which many of us spend significant time, find meaning, and form identities (Ashmore, Deaux & McLaughlin-Volpe, 2004; Dutton, Roberts & Bednar, 2010; Pratt, Rockmann & Kaufmann, 2006). It is a place that inspires, but can also be unconducive to wellbeing (McQuaid & Kern, 2017). We are fully aware of the present-day pressures on higher education and the shifts that have occurred; one of these has been the rise in the expectation of working with others and collaborating successfully across all areas of the role. As early career researchers and doctoral students, this expectation is very much assumed.

Collaboration can empower some of us, and for others it can be something that makes us want to run and avoid at all costs. Varying lived experiences can inform these feelings.

Let's look at a framework that might be able to support you to think about all the big picture complexities of working with others, that is PERMAH (we mentioned this briefly in Chapter 3). PERMAH builds off the work of Seligman's (2011) PERMA framework, with the H added by McQuaid and Kern (2017) to acknowledge the importance of health in viewing wellbeing (Table 4.1). The framework provides a roadmap to wellbeing, offering a way for individuals and systems (Huppert & So, 2013) to 'understand, measure and take action using evidence based research tools' (McQuaid & Kern, 2017, p. 13). Let's look at each of these pillars.

Positive emotions

Positive emotions (e.g., hope or openness) broaden and build ways to respond to opportunities and challenges

Table 4.1 Thinking and working with others

	Wellbeing framework	Examples of strengths alignment when thinking about collaborations and working with others	Examples of skills that might be associated
P	Positive emotions: Experiencing positive feelings	Curiosity Hope Gratitude Kindness Love Humour	Smiling Making eye contact Sharing an appreciation Bringing energy Authenticity Tolerance Dealing with others' anger Cooling off Noticing others' strengths Expressing empathy Saying 'Thank you'
E	Engagement: Being interested and involved in life. Experiencing flow.	Fairness Creativity Zest	Attention to detail Offering other ways of approaching a task Organisation Begining a conversation Ignoring distractions Following directions

Collaboration skills and strengths 83

Wellbeing framework		Examples of strengths alignment when thinking about collaborations and working with others	Examples of skills that might be associated
R	Relationships: Connections with other people. Feeling loved and valued.	Perspective Honesty Social intelligence Teamwork Humility Forgiveness Leadership	Making connections Communication Being on time Offering feedback Being supportive Attention to detail Maintaining minutes Note taking Listening Connecting via social media Checking in on others Investing in time with others Reliability Compromise Convincing others Taking responsibility Taking turns Joining in Knowing when to change approach

(Continued)

Table 4.1 Continued

Wellbeing framework	Examples of strengths alignment when thinking about collaborations and working with others	Examples of skills that might be associated
M	Meaning: Connecting to something bigger than ourselves. Having a sense of direction. Feeling valuable and worthwhile.	Judgement Bravery Love of learning	Writing Stepping back and reflecting before responding Visually mapping links Including others Bringing on others to a team Making connections Building from failure
A	Accomplishment: Having a sense of mastery. Feeling as though you have achieved a goal. Ability and belief that what you do matters.	Perseverance Prudence Appreciation of beauty and excellence	Meeting deadlines Chunking your time Planning Mapping timelines Hosting events Sending an acknowledgement note Promoting achievements
H	Health: Physical health.	Fairness Self-regulation Spirituality	Taking breaks Arranging social events Offering support and feedback Finding time to exercise Bringing healthy snacks

(Fredrickson, 2001). In the workplace, these have been attributed to improving job satisfaction and relationships, and experiencing success (McQuaid & Kern, 2017). Both negative and positive emotions can be experienced simultaneously (Watson & Tellegen, 1985), and offer opportunities for growth and adding value to life outcomes (Butler & Kern 2016; Howell, Kern & Lyubomirsky, 2007; Lyubomirsky et al., 2005).

Engagement

The focus of engagement in positive psychology has been on flow, centred on intense concentration, absorption, and focus (Csikszentmihalyi, 1990). This, as McQuaid and Kern (2017) note, is in relation to being fully absorbed in what one is doing, and connected to experiencing a stronger sense of self, feeling more self-belief, and experiencing higher levels of confidence. Experiencing engagement in the workplace comes from clear goals balanced with skill level, sense of autonomy, choice in approach, and feedback.

Relationships

Relationships are fundamental to life (Berscheid & Reis, 1998; Seligman, 2011). In the workplace relationships influence identity (Gecas, 1982; Gergen, 1994), this includes seeking social support and work-based friendships (Berman, West, & Richter, 2002; Dutton & Ragins, 2007). Although there is no research consensus of how a positive work identity is maintained (Dutton et al., 2010), there are many influences, including: how individuals construct a positive work-related identity as they develop in a career; how one is motivated or maintains a positive focus when feeling isolated; or how one overcomes physical, moral, or social taints to create a positive sense of self at work (Dutton et al., 2010; Kreiner, Ashforth & Sluss, 2006).

Meaning

Meaning provides a sense that one's life matters, and that one can make a difference to others (Butler & Kern, 2016; McQuaid & Kern, 2017; Seligman, 2011). There is a sense of purpose to what one does (Steger, 2012). Meaning has been linked to both better physical health and higher life satisfaction (Boyle et al., 2009; Steger, 2012). For many, meaning, including self-definition and identity, is closely connected to work (Ashforth & Mael, 1989; Carlsen, 2008; Dutton et al., 2010; Gini, 1998; Stryker & Serpe, 1994), and is reformed and transformed (Ashmore et al., 2004; Pratt, Rockmann & Kaufmann, 2006; Smith, 2017).

Accomplishment

Accomplishment can mean different things to each individual in the workplace – for some, it is about an achievement (e.g., award or promotion) (McQuaid & Kern, 2017); for others, it can be subjective (e.g., reaching goals or completion of tasks) (Butler & Kern, 2016). From a wellbeing perspective, McQuaid and

Kern (2017) remind us that 'it is the small, subjective wins that matter most' (p. 113).

Health

Maintaining physical health, including eating well, movement, sleep, and mindful restoration activities are behaviours that support wellbeing, including mental health, relationships, and cognitive functioning (Blake et al., 2009; McQuaid & Kern, 2017). In the workplace, the place of health is gaining increased attention, acknowledging that there needs to be shifts in workplace culture to support employees (Malik, Blake & Suggs, 2013).

Working collaboratively with others

What might mindfulness and strengths-based outlooks mean for working collaboratively with others? In Table 4.1 we unpack how strengths and skills might be linked to working collaboratively. This is a starting point to consider this way of working and we acknowledge this can appear different to any of us.

McQuaid and Kern (2017) remind us that for each person, tools and approaches will vary, depending on the person, situation, individual and collective states of wellbeing, and the outcomes wanting to be achieved (pp. 13–20). So, when working with your partners the key is knowing yourself, and then knowing how you can work with others (knowing their strengths and being able to spot them). We'll connect with this in the case studies as this chapter progresses.

Approaching collaborations from a bigger context of spreading good academic behaviour: *Circle of Niceness*

What can strengths in relation to collaborations look like in practice? Narelle's colleague Rachel Pitt, in conversation with Inger Mewburn and Stuart Palmer (Mewburn, 2013), coined the term '*Circle of Niceness*' back in 2013 and this has been a way of being that has resonated greatly for her as a way of being in navigating higher education. In thinking more about the concept, Narelle blogged about this in 2018 (Lemon, 2018) as a way to begin to articulate what it is to spread good academic behaviour sourcing feedback via Twitter and colleagues as part of a WhisperCon unconference session (Khoo & O'Donnell, 2018). You'll be able to see the strengths language emerging in this mapping (see Figure 4.1).

Circle of Niceness is a phase that is underpinned by mutual respect. It is embodied. When you are engaged in a *Circle of Niceness* you are collegial in all senses of being – you support, develop trust, admire, are curious, honest, grateful, kind and build a genuine relationship with others. The language of strengths-based work, which we have covered in this and the previous chapter, comes into play here. For example, we are collegial and show a huge amount of reciprocity and gratitude for one another on many levels. We display warmth. And there is a genuine mutual respect in the relationship and opportunity is afforded to learn from one another. It is embodied and enacted with others, those in your circle of people who both give and receive these actions.

Collaboration skills and strengths 89

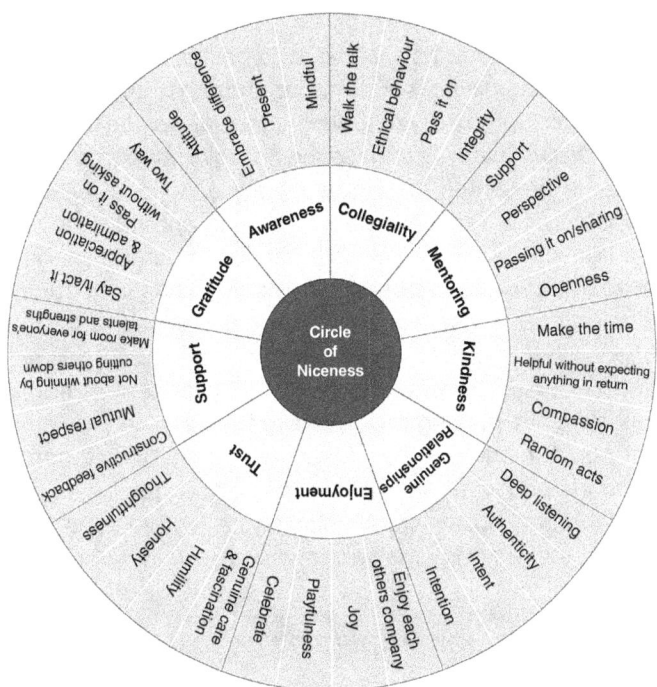

Figure 4.1 The *Circle of Niceness*.

In higher education we are encouraged to collaborate; as a part of this, consideration is made both to how we participate and present oneself while also to considering who it is we work with. Sometimes we have choices; on other occasions we do not. But when it comes to how we can approach a collaboration we always have the opportunity to embody and model good academic behaviour. How do you want to be treated? What do we value? We acknowledge there can be different levels of interactions with others, and yes there is so often undesirable behaviour that is directed towards us or observed. However, our awareness around how we want to be has a huge impact on the relationships we form, our and other experiences, and opportunity. If, by embodying the values of a *Circle of Niceness* as one way to describe collegial support, opportunity is presented to shift what our academic relationships can be. This enables a rethinking and reframing of our relationships with more connection to our values, purpose, meaning, and positive emotions. Being with others who embody these elements provides one with a feeling of positivity, a 'glow' if you like, as there is a mutual respect and genuine curiosity and admiration for talking about ideas we are working on, decoding the job, and providing support for one another. Openness and honesty come hand in hand with *Circle of Niceness*. As we navigate our way through academia, we also find a way to hang with people that embody the values you believe in.

Cases and examples

Let's work with our case studies. These case studies illustrate ways people in different situations might distinguish individual roles in association to strengths and skills while providing supporting strategies for individuals to unpack each of these areas. Do you identify with any of them?

Let's assume **Elizabeth** has a strength of Hope. With this strength illuminated she is energised and finds it naturally rewarding to expect the best in the future. She works to achieve this. Her skill set of listening and being able

to connect to her vision and goals enables her to approach this situation with an awareness of what she would like to achieve. In this situation, she is honing her strength in finding a way to work with a new research team that enables her to find her place. Although she is working with senior researchers, there is an opportunity to model and embrace her strength of hope. She would approach this by articulating what she is experiencing currently, framing an inquiry around posing questions such as: How do you see me contributing to this project? What can I bring to support the project? How can we work together to make this happen?

The strength of zest enables **Phillipe** to approach a co-writing opportunity with excitement and energy. He knows his PhD topic well and is now in a situation where he is learning a new genre of writing; how to write for a journal article. By pairing his zest with skills of knowing the topic and willingness to learn he can think about how to have conversations with his PhD supervisors about how to approach this new writing task. He might ask the questions: What is a model of journal structure that I could utilise? What specific area of my PhD findings could we focus on? What might this look like in outlining this in a new format such as a journal paper? What aspects of my PhD writing could I use in the journal paper? How could we approach this as a collaboration?

The opportunity to learn new things is **Jesse's** strength. They have a love of learning in both formal and self-directed settings. This strength puts them in good stead to negotiate how building a trajectory as an early career researcher can support them. Paired with the strength of humility (not seeking the spotlight, preferring to let your accomplishments speak for themselves and valuing your modesty), this affords them the opportunity to seek out advice from more experienced academics in how to approach their situation. The skills associated with asking sincere questions, and being curious (also a strength) sets them up to be able to seek out advice and approach advice by asking the questions: Can I please show you my CV and profile to talk through how I might approach developing my trajectory? What next steps could I undertake? What is possible? How do I work smartly by leveraging the teaching I am doing?

As **Alicia** scopes out how she can contribute to both her postdoctoral team projects and her own aligned projects, she is able to use her strength of social intelligence (being aware of the motives and feelings of other people, and being able to negotiate this across different social situations (in this case her university and stakeholder colleagues) while also knowing what to do to put others at ease). Her skill set of being organised and ability

> to plan at the micro and macro levels allows for opportunity to connect in others while also positioning herself for growth and focus in the work to energise her. She might ask the questions: How could the focus area in which I am interested align to the ideas I have about projects I could lead? How could others be a part of this? What might be opportunities to learn from others and the strengths they have to contribute to success?

Now we invite you to take these examples and put them into practice. In doing this, consider putting into practice a key awareness strategy connected to reflection in action.

As you work with your strengths and skills and the contexts in which you work, we have developed an approach to thinking about strengths and skills with your partners using the Taxonomy of Collaboration (see Appendix 1). We have offered these as a way for you to also think through these concepts given your own situations.

Into practice

Now that we have worked with the case studies and you are beginning to think about your own situation, we offer a strategy to support the integration of these principles as a way to assist blockers or obstacles that may emerge for you. We connect with awareness and reflection in action.

When working with others there are times when you need to reconsider or (re)frame where you are coming from – What is an alternative question I could ask? How might I (re)frame a question? What extra knowledge could I have planned for? What different approach could I have taken to support me being able to communicate where I was coming from? And in your reflections of being a doctoral or early career researcher there are always moments you can rethink an approach or how a discussion was carried out. Reflection in action (Schön, 1983) means to think about, or reflect, while you are carrying out the activity. It occurs in the moment, for example embracing a question, or picking up on a sharing moment that could provide opportunity in the moment to enhance learning or embracing a challenge that emerges. It is these elements that mark the difference of reflection in action to reflection on action, that occurs after you have engaged in a conversation or event. Reflection in action sparks questions such as:

- Now what can I do?
- Now what do I need to do?
- Now what might I do to improve or enhance the situation?
- How can I take a moment to regroup and be in the present moment with openness?
- Now what might be the consequences of this change in collaboration focus or conversation?
- What opportunities arise?
- Now what might I change?
- Now what might I pick up on?
- Now what is on offer in this learning moment for me?
- Now what is on offer in this learning moment for the partners?
- What can I do if things go wrong?

Aligning your strengths

In both this chapter and Chapter 2, we have written about how important it is to partner with those who have different strengths. But what happens when we work with someone who has the same strengths as you but uses them differently? When you work with someone who shares your strengths, it can be easy to assume they think and act like you do. The key to this situation is finding where your differences lie and how this can make both of you even stronger. Key to this situation is:

- Noticing how colleague works.
- Seeking feedback and constructive review.
- Drawing on your language of strengths to learn from one another.
- Not making assumptions that you utilise the strength in the same way, acknowledging that this is when skills come into play in action.
- Openness and curiosity to different approaches.
- Ongoing dialogue about approaches.
- Being careful not to overuse your strength.
- Considering how you can pair your strength with other strengths.
- Viewing approaches as being complementary, rather than in competition.

What could go wrong?

There are times when we have taken all the right steps and worked in a proactive manner – but things still go awry. In a group collaboration, two common problems can jeopardise the project: freeloaders and miscommunication. Let's look at the issues and tactics you can try. Also, refer to Chapter 8 for more problem-solving options, as well as strategies and reflective questions we have posed throughout each of the chapters.

Free riders

The term *free riders* refers to the situation that arises when one or more partners does not fully complete their part of the workload. The problem is exacerbated when the group feels that someone is falling short on the work, but will receive the same recognition or reward that others merit from hard work (Saghafian & O'Neill, 2018). Certainly, there are times when personal issues arise, and the partner needs extra time or help. But when someone is simply shirking the work that has been agreed upon, resentment can build. Here are a few strategies to help address this problem:

- Communicate one-to-one with the individual to discern the nature of the obstruction and adjust timing or deliverables. Initiate communication sooner rather than later, because the longer the problem persists, the more damage it can cause (Hall & Buzwell, 2012). Sometimes when we fall behind or run into an obstacle, we might delay communicating with partners, which might be the case. A message, 'Do you need a couple more days to finish this work?' or 'Can I help you move this forward?' might motivate your partner to move forward.
- If that does not work… call a meeting, face-to-face, videoconference or phone conference as a team.

Review agreements about deliverables, expectations, and timelines. Adjust as needed. Reassign tasks or offer more flexibility for completing tasks. If that does not work…
- Work in a 'buddy system' rather than breaking a large project into pieces each individual completes. Research shows that smaller teams experience fewer problems with free riders (Albanese & Van Fleet, 1985).
- If the collaboration has external stakeholders, a principal investigator, project manager, or supervisor, include them in written communications with the free rider. Ask for advice or support. If that does not work…
- If the partner is not contributing, and will not communicate about how to remedy the problem, you may need to ask the individual to step away from the project.

Communication and dialogue

Communication and listening are key when we are problem-solving. We must commit to being our best and modelling ideal communication behaviours. While we are accustomed to text messaging, emails, and posts, face-to-face or other real-time communications might be best when we are trying to solve a problem or de-escalate a conflict. Informal one-to-one communication can be important when the missing person is not responding to formal group messages (Jeong, Choi, & Kim, 2014).

There are different ways we can communicate. We summarise four of them in Table 4.2. Try to place yourself in the active, constructive type when responding to disagreements or to addressing shortcomings from other partners. This communication style plays a large part in

Table 4.2 Communication response matrix

	Active	Passive
Constructive	Authentic Enthusiastic and open Eye contact Smiling Positive body language High energy	Low energy Quiet Delayed response Limited eye contact Body language that is shut off
Deconstructive	Dismissive Aggressive Demeaning Reactionary	Avoid Turn inward Focus on negative self-talk Ignore speaker

relationship building and is connected to commitment, satisfaction, intimacy, and trust (Gable et al., 2004). As such, it offers the potential to heal rifts that can emerge in a group project.

Another aspect that can support you are Erich Fromm's guidelines of listening (Popova, 2017). These offer some helpful insights regarding the mindset that we can adopt in approaching communication. Placed at the heart of this approach is active listening and mindful awareness. We have reframed these guidelines as:

- When we approach a situation where we need to communicate, we need to be present, in the moment. So, nothing beyond the matter at hand must be on your mind, and you must be optimally free from anxiety as well as from greed.

- Be open. You must possess a freely-working imagination which is sufficiently concrete to be expressed in words.
- Hold the space of compassion (being able to see from another's point of view and be open to action, moving forward or negotiating and seeing other perspectives). You must be endowed with a capacity for empathy with another person and strong enough to feel the experience of the other as if it were his/her own.
- Embrace compassion. The condition for such empathy is a crucial facet of the capacity for love. To understand another means to love him/her/them – not in the erotic sense, but in the sense of reaching out to him/her/them and of overcoming the fear of losing oneself.
- Understand. Understanding and loving are inseparable. If they are separate, it is a cerebral process and the door to essential understanding remains closed.

Try it! Exercises and questions for discussion or reflection

As you move forward exploring your strengths and skills and applying these to your collaborative situation, we invite you to consider this situation:

You are collaborating on an important team project. You know one of the partners, but don't know the two others. One is part-time, and prefers to meet virtually. You must work with your partners to synthesise their ideas and plan, organise and complete the creation of a presentation. This presentation should meld all contributions into a collective final product.

- What steps will you take to get acquainted with partners you don't know? How will you build trust within the group?
- How will you communicate and meet?
- If some can meet in person and one is not co-located, how can you avoid leaving out the member who can only meet virtually?
- How will you organise the project to utilise strengths of each member?
- What will success look like? How will you measure or assess it?
- What ways of working should you put in place?
- What steps will you take to establish and maintain trust?
- What strengths can you call upon to approach this context?

Take it away

In this chapter we have explored how you can work with your strengths and skills in a collaborative context. We encourage the use of strengths-based language with positivity, awareness, and openness to support a mindful approach. You have had the opportunity to consider with the case examples, as well as connect with some practical strategies to support best practice and times when obstacles may occur. We now invite you to think about how build from these suggestions while also enacting your own *Circle of Niceness*.

References

Albanese, R., & Van Fleet, D. (1985). The free riding tendency in organizations. *Scandinavian Journal of Management Studies*, 2, 121–136. doi:10.1016/0281-7527(85)90003-9

Ashforth, B. E., & Mael, F. (1989). Social identity theory and the organization. *Academy of Management Review*, *14*, 20–39.

Ashmore, R., Deaux, K., & McLaughlin-Volpe, T. (2004). An organizing framework for collective identity: Articulation and significance of multidimensionality. *Psychological Bulletin*, *130*, 80–114.

Berman, E., West, J. P., & Richter, M. N. (2002). Workplace relations: Friendship patterns and consequences (according to managers). *Public Administration Review*, *62*, 217–230.

Berscheid, E., & Reis, H. T. (1998). Attraction and close relationships. In D. T. Gilbert, S. T. Fiske & G. Lindzey (Eds.), *The handbook of social psychology* (pp. 193–281). New York, NY: McGraw-Hill.

Blake, H., Mo, P., Malik, S., & Thomas, S. (2009). How effective are physical activity interventions for alleviating depressive symptoms in older people? A systematic review. *Clinical Rehabilitation*, *23*, 873–887.

Boyle, P. A., Barnes, L. L., Buchman, A. S., & Bennett, D. A. (2009). Purpose in life is associated with mortality among community-dwelling older persons. *Psychosomatic Medicine*, *71*(5), 574-579.

Butler, J., & Kern, M. L. (2016). The PERMA-Profiler: A brief multidimensional measure of flourishing. *International Journal of Wellbeing*, *6*(3), 1–48.

Carlsen, A. (2008). Positive dramas: Enacting self-adventures in organizations. *Journal of Positive Psychology*, *3*, 55–75.

Csikszentmihalyi, M. (1990). *Flow: The psychology of optimal experience*. New York, NY: Harper and Row.

Dutton, J. E., & Ragins, B. (2007). *Exploring positive relationships at work: Building a theoretical and research foundation*. Mahwah, NJ: Lawrence Erlbaum Associates.

Dutton, J. E., Roberts, L. M., & Bednar, J. (2010). Pathways for positive identity construction at work: Four types of positive identity and the building of social resources. *Academy of Management Review*, *35*(2), 265–293.

Fredrickson, B. L. (2001). The role of positive emotions in positive psychology: The broaden-and build theory of positive emotions. *American Psychologist*, *56*, 218–226.

Gable, S. L., Reis, H. T., Impett, E. A., & Asher, E. R. (2004). What do you do when things go right? The intrapersonal and interpersonal benefits of sharing positive events. *Journal of Personality and Social Psychology*, *87*(2), 228.

Gecas, V. (1982). The self-concept. *Annual Review of Sociology*, *8*, 1–33.

Gergen, K. J. (1994). *Realities and relationships: Soundings in social construction*. Boston: Harvard University Press.

Gini, A. (1998). Work, identity and self: How we are formed by the work we do. *Journal of Business Ethics*, *17*, 707–714.

Hall, D., & Buzwell, S. (2012). The problem of free-riding in group projects: Looking beyond social loafing as reason for non-contribution. *Active Learning in Higher Education*, *14*(1), 37–49. doi:10.1177/1469787412467123

Howard, L. W. (1998). Validating the competing values model as a representation of organizational cultures. *The International Journal of Organizational Analysis*, *6*(3), 231–250.

Howell, R., Kern, M. L., & Lyubomirsky, S. (2007). Health benefits: Meta-analytically determining the impact of well-being on objective health outcomes. *Health Psychology Review*, *1*(1), 83–136.

Huppert, F. A., & So, T. T. C. (2013). Flourishing across Europe: Application of a new conceptual framework for defining well-being. *Social Indicators Research*, *110*(3), 837–861.

Jeong, S., Choi, J. Y., & Kim, J.-Y. (2014). On the drivers of international collaboration: The impact of informal communication, motivation, and research resources. *Science & Public Policy (SPP)*, *41*(4), 520–531. doi:10.1093/scipol/sct079

Khoo, T., & O'Donnell, J. (2018). The Whisper Workshop: New ways to connect, new ideas for research. Retrieved from https://researchwhisperer.org/presentations/2018-whisper-workshop/

Kreiner, G., Ashforth, B., & Sluss, D. (2006). Identity dynamics in occupational dirty work: Integrating social identity and system justification perspectives. *Organization Science*, *17*, 619–636.

Lemon, N. (2018). Circle of niceness: mapping our values. Retrieved from https://chatwithrellypops.wordpress.com/2018/09/18/circle-of-niceness-mapping-our-values

Lyubomirsky, S., King, L. A., & Diener, E. (2005). The benefits of frequent positive affect: Does happiness lead to success? *Psychological Bulletin*, *131*(6), 803–855.

Malik, S. M., Blake, H., & Suggs, L. S. (2013). A systematic review of workplace health promotion interventions for increasing physical activity. *British Journal of Health Psychology*, *19*(1), 149–180.

McQuaid, M., & Kern, P. (2017). *Your wellbeing blueprint: Feeling good and doing well at work*. Melbourne: Michelle McQuaid.

Mewburn, I. (2013). Academic assholes and the circle of niceness. Retrieved from https://thesiswhisperer.com/2013/02/13/academic-assholes/

Popova, M. (2017). Erich Fromm's 6 rules of listening: The great humanistic philosopher and psychologist on the art of unselfish understanding. Retrieved from https://www.brainpickings.org/2017/04/05/erich-fromm-the-art-of-listening/

Pratt, M. G., Rockmann, K. W., & Kaufmann, J. B. (2006). Constructing professional identity: The role of work and identity learning cycles in the customization of identity among medical residents. *Academy of Management Journal*, *49*, 235–262.

Saghafian, M., & O'Neill, D. K. (2018). A phenomenological study of teamwork in online and face-to-face student teams. *Higher Education*, *75*(1), 57–73. doi:10.1007/s10734-017-0122-4

Schein, E. (1990). Organizational culture. *American Psychologist*, *45*(2), 109–119.

Schön, D. A. (1983). *The reflective practitioner: How professionals think in action*. New York: Basic Books.

Seligman, M. E. P. (2011). *Flourish. A visionary new understanding of happiness and well-being*. New York: Free Press.

Smith, E. E. (2017). *The power of meaning crafting a life that matters*. New York, NY: Random House.

Steger, M. F. (2012). Experiencing meaning in life: Optimal functioning at the nexus of spirituality, psychopathology, and wellbeing. In P. T. P. Wong (Ed.), *The human quest for meaning* (pp. 165–184). New York, NY: Routledge.

Stryker, S., & Serpe, R. T. (1994). Identity salience and psychological centrality: Equivalent, overlapping, or complementary concepts? *Social Psychology Quarterly*, *57*, 16–35.

Watson, D., & Tellegen, A. (1985). Toward a consensual structure of mood. *Psychological Bulletin*, *98*(2), 219-235.

5 Collaboration and teaching and learning

What will you learn by studying this chapter?

As a new academic, you might have teaching responsibilities. In these roles you might find that you need to look at two angles: your own collaborative relationships with other faculty and staff, and the collaborative learning experiences of your students. This chapter looks at the collaboration process in regard to teaching and learning in the higher education context. Tips are offered to support early career researchers and doctoral students working in these situations in online and face-to-face settings.

In this chapter you will gain an understanding of:

- Using collaborative course assignments or projects to prepare for collaboration in professional settings.
- Preparing for roles as instructors who teach with collaborative methods.
- Analysing ways to support collaborative learning.
- Identifying opportunities to learn collaboratively as a new professional.

The big picture: What is collaborative learning?

A definition of collaboration was introduced in Chapter 1:

> Collaboration is an interactive process that engages two or more participants who work together to achieve outcomes they could not accomplish independently.
> (Salmons, 2019, p. 5)

In collaborative learning, the interactive process has a purposeful learning goal. Students work together not only to achieve outcomes, but also to develop greater understanding. Others, including the instructor, resource people, and experts from the community beyond the class, may also be a part of the collaborative learning activity. Let's define *collaborative learning* as:

> Constructing knowledge, negotiating meanings, and/or solving problems through mutual engagement of two or more students in a coordinated effort.
> (Salmons, 2019, p. 5)

The terms "teamwork" and "collaboration" are closely related, but they are not precisely synonymous. Teams may use either collaborative or individual work to accomplish shared goals. While students may complete parts of a project independently, when they coordinate their efforts to generate new ideas or find the answers to problems, we can describe their work as "collaboration". Trust is essential to successful collaboration, and to collaborative learning.

Learning and teaching can be face-to-face, blended, or online. What might collaborative e-learning look like? The term *e-learning* describes entire degree programmes, courses, or seminars that are offered entirely online. In online or hybrid classes interaction between students and instructors occurs electronically. Online students interact through discussions and activities involving the whole class, small groups or dyads. In hybrid or blended learning, online activities complement face-to-face meetings.

Here we'll define collaborative e-learning as:

> Constructing knowledge, negotiating meanings and/or solving problems through mutual engagement of two or more students in a coordinated effort using Internet and electronic communications.

In a face-to-face classroom we can draw on both verbal and nonverbal approaches to exchange messages. In an online or blended learning class, by contrast, we use technologies to communicate synchronously, asynchronously, or both. Information and communication technologies (ICTs) and learning management platforms allow us to communicate using text, audio, video, or a combination of these three approaches. E-learning offers an ideal opportunity to learn and practice ways to work together and think collaboratively.

Throughout this chapter, we invite you to think about your own learning experiences in school, college, and/or university. Did you have opportunities to learn collaboratively, and, if so, did you find them beneficial? Why do you think those collaborations were successful? Was it the people, the instructors' support and guidance, or the way the assignment was organised? If you encountered problems in completing assignments collaboratively, think about ways the strategies introduced here might help to alleviate such problems.

What theories and models help us to design collaborative learning experiences?

Bloom's Taxonomy

The first theory and model to consider is Bloom's *Taxonomy of Educational Objectives for the Cognitive Domain.* Commonly known simply as 'Bloom's Taxonomy,' this is a framework that shows six levels of thinking, from knowledge through evaluation (Bloom, Engelhart, Furst, Hill, & Krathwohl, 1956). In 2000, some of the original writers and new researchers updated their work to reflect changes in the ways we think about knowledge and information (Anderson, Bloom, Krathwohl, & Airasian, 2000).

One of the most significant changes was in the newly articulated *Knowledge Dimension*. In Table 5.1, you can see how the writers differentiated types of knowledge. The first, *factual knowledge*, is the simplest and the most likely to be acquired through individual learning activities. *Conceptual knowledge*, which entails grasping relationships between ideas, theories, principles, and/or applications, lends itself to collaborative learning. Sometimes interacting with others and hearing their perspectives helps us see relationships that might otherwise be hidden. *Procedural knowledge* is essential for collaborative learning as well as collaborative projects. This is the 'how-to' type of knowledge. We might have all the facts, and be open to new conceptual frameworks, but not know how to organise efforts that involve collaborative partners.

Table 5.1 Knowledge dimensions in Bloom's Taxonomy revision

Knowledge dimensions
Factual knowledge: The basic elements that students must know to be acquainted with a discipline or solve problems in it.
Conceptual knowledge: Interrelationships among the basic elements within a larger structure that enable them to function together.
Procedural knowledge: How to do something; methods of inquiry, and criteria for using skills.
Metacognitive knowledge: Knowledge of cognition in general as well as awareness and knowledge of one's own cognition.

As you reflect on your own learning experiences and the kinds of assignments and projects, you'd like to offer your own students, consider ways that learning the skills necessary to collaborate successfully as a type of procedural knowledge. *Metacognitive knowledge* is the final piece of the puzzle. This is the mindful reflection component. What does it all mean?

Let's dig more deeply into knowledge dimensions of collaboration with the next theoretical model, the Collaborative Knowledge Learning Model.

The Collaborative Knowledge Learning Model (Salmons, 2019)

When assignments or research projects are designed for completion by collaborative partners, the objective is for

Collaboration and teaching and learning 109

peers to learn from and with each other. This can occur to a variety of degrees, so it's important to be clear about what you want to achieve, depending on the nature of the academic setting and characteristics of the students (see Figure 5.1).

In other words, if we both have pieces of relevant articles that will benefit our project, sharing them can be described as *knowledge exchange*. As instructors, we encourage a culture of generosity and reciprocity to promote knowledge exchange. This is also where utilising strengths can support the process, especially with strengths spotting in each other. In this way a common language begins to emerge and also support partner cohesion.

If I am an expert at something that you need to know about to complete our project, I can coach or mentor you to transfer what I know so you can learn from it. This can be described as *knowledge transfer*. As instructors, you need to understand your students' strengths and assign project groups accordingly.

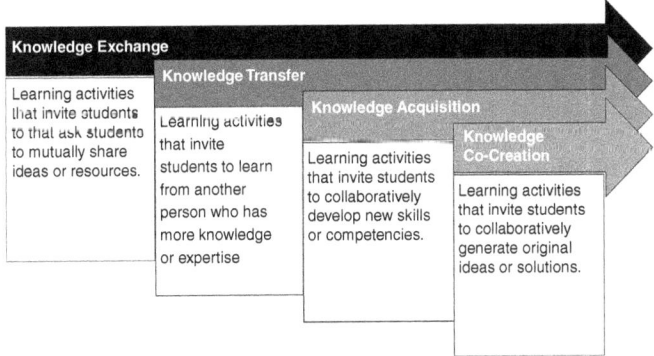

Figure 5.1 Collaborative Knowledge Learning Model.

If we need to learn something that is new to both of us to complete our project, we can use *knowledge acquisition* to learn it together. As instructors, again, we need to know students' strengths and areas where new learning needs to occur. We need to allow time and provide guidance or instruction so they can learn whatever is needed to complete the project.

If we work together to use what we've learned to create new ideas or solutions, we can use *knowledge co-creation*. When students interpret course materials to write a paper, or give a presentation, they gain experience with knowledge co-creation.

This is not a linear model, and a given project might involve multiple knowledge learning stages.

As you think about your own learning experiences and the kinds of assignments and projects you'd like to offer your own students, think about times you have exchanged, transferred, acquired, or co-created new ideas with others. What assignments or projects engaged you in learning new knowledge? What instructional practices helped?

The Taxonomy of Collaboration

The Taxonomy of Collaboration was introduced in Chapter 1. It has six elements. Three are processes used by nearly all collaborations: reflection, dialogue, and review. The other three describe work design options: parallel, sequential, or synergistic approaches used by groups to complete the task or project. In Figure 5.2, these approaches are described in the context of teaching and learning.

Most collaborations will include a mix of these elements. The savvy group thinks strategically, agrees to a

Collaboration and teaching and learning 111

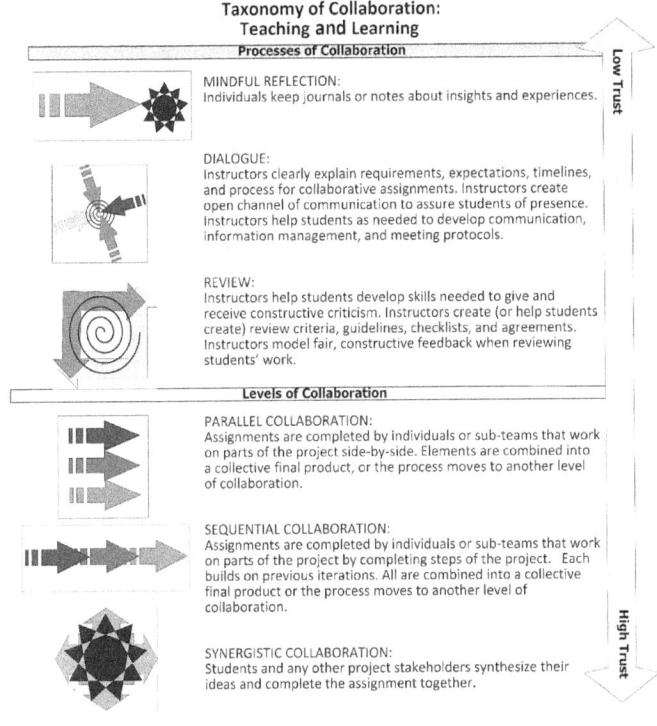

Figure 5.2 Applying the Taxonomy of Collaboration for instruction.

plan that incorporates mindful reflection, dialogue, and review stages, and organises work to be completed in a fair and accountable way. The essential glue that holds these elements together is trust.

The Taxonomy of Collaboration builds on the work of Bloom and others who have developed taxonomies for educational purposes. When an educator creates a learning experience drawing on Bloom's Taxonomy, students can achieve two broad goals: (1) acquiring competencies in the content area; and (2) learning critical thinking and knowledge development skills. When an educator creates a learning experience with the Taxonomy of Collaboration as a guide, students can achieve goals of: acquiring factual and conceptual competencies in the content area, and procedural skills in communication, shared leadership, decision-making, team and group process.

Cases and examples

Let's connect with our cases:

Phillipe is new to teaching and is in a contract position. In this role, he has little opportunity to develop new courses or instructional approaches. However, he is using class discussion time for small-group activities he thinks will help students learn from each other.

Alicia's postdoc includes assisting with a large lecture course, along with three other postdocs. She cannot collaborate with the professor given that it is their course, and they have a system in place for teaching it. However, she is collaborating with the other postdocs to develop and share resources. At first everyone worked in parallel to create supplementary material for each week's lecture, but without coordination or shared purpose, she didn't feel it was a collaborative effort. She organised a meeting where they worked synergistically to develop a template and consistent elements to include in each resource. They agreed to meet at the end of the term and put all of the resources together in a workbook-like document for students to use the next time this course is offered.

Jesse has been assigned one large introductory course, and one seminar. The course is currently lecture-based, and the seminar is discussion-oriented. The field of study is one that leads to a team-based work life. They plan to revise both after the first year to include more collaborative projects that prepare students for professional success. An intention has been created that opportunity arises to work collaboratively with more experienced faculty when they update the course.

Elizabeth is in a position where she needs to work collaboratively with other research and programme/degree staff. However, the agency has been through a lot of staffing turnover, and others are distrustful about working together. Before launching into any initiative or project, she is meeting with each person on a one-to-one basis, and trying to build trust, and to identify individual and collective strengths.

How would you move forward in the situations faced by Phillipe, Alicia, Jesse, and Elizabeth? What other ways can they use and build strengths as collaborative partners, and as advocates for building collective strengths with others?

Into practice: Preparing to teach collaboratively

As a teaching assistant, intern, early career researcher, casual academic, or new faculty member you have a chance to help prepare today's students for life and work in a digitally-connected world. When you incorporate collaborative approaches into both the content and context of educational activities, your students will have the opportunity to learn from and with each other while they develop skills that will be beneficial to them now and in the future.

Why should I be thinking about collaborative learning now?

Academic and professional life in the digital age requires a different set of strategic, cross-cultural, team and technical skills than did the face-to-face, locally based operations of the past. Today's students need 21st-century skills that will allow them to work collaboratively across boundaries of geography, time, and culture as well as across disciplines.

Online communication for social purposes has become pervasive. Whether using a computer on a desk or a mobile device on the go, people seem to be almost seamlessly connected. But do they know how to leverage such connections to generate unique and valuable results?

Can they translate the skills used for casual exchange into skills needed for complex cross-cultural collaboration? Or will they work with others whose knowledge basis, world views, agendas, ways of thinking, and decision-making are entirely unfamiliar? If you are conversant in emerging collaborative approaches to education and training, you can make a genuine contribution to a department where you are serving. You will be able to better prepare students to be a part of in a continually changing and highly diverse environment.

How can I support collaborative learning, both off- and online?

In a face-to-face classroom we can draw on both verbal and nonverbal approaches to exchange messages. In an online or blended learning class, we use technologies to communicate synchronously, asynchronously, or both. Information and communication technologies (ICTs) and learning management platforms allow us to communicate using text, audio, video, or a combination of these three approaches.

How can I design and plan assignments for students to complete collaboratively?

Clearly, when using collaborative instructional approaches, we must think about process and delivery, not just the content of a course, seminar, or training module. The three models described in this chapter help us think through how and why to use collaborative learning approaches when we take an instructional role: Bloom's Taxonomy

(Anderson et al., 2000; Bloom et al., 1956), the Collaborative Knowledge Learning Model (Salmons, 2019), and the Taxonomy of Collaboration (Salmons, 2019).

To start with the knowledge learning model, we must determine not only what knowledge we hope students will come away with, but also what strengths exist in the group. Are there stronger, more experienced students who can exchange or transfer knowledge with others? Or will they all need to acquire new knowledge together? The level of trust, and need for adequate time, and the ability to make decisions and coordinate a project will vary depending on whether you simply want students to share ideas, or you want them to generate an outcome they create together. All collaborative assignments involve interdependencies and shared decision-making. However, Parallel and Sequential Teams need to negotiate on more procedural bases, whereas Synergistic Teams must negotiate and collaborate on a more conceptual level.

We can integrate all three conceptual models. See Table 5.2 for examples, and think about how you and your students negotiate knowledge domains in collaborative projects.

As you think the assignments and projects you'd like to offer your own students, think about the approaches that can make collaborative learning interesting and fun. What might this look like?

How can I use collaborative learning approaches to gain skills on the job?

The situation is the same but different from the classroom setting, when you are trying to learn from others on the job. When you are a new intern, teaching assistant,

Table 5.2 Using conceptual models for instruction

Knowledge domain	Taxonomy of Collaboration	Knowledge learning
Factual knowledge	Dialogue to determine what facts and foundations will inform the project. When research is needed for background or contextual information, plan to collaborate using parallel, sequential, or synergistic work designs. Review each other's work for accuracy.	*Knowledge exchange:* Share facts and background research important to the project. *Knowledge transfer:* Coach or guide collaborative partners to access and use foundational knowledge in new project. *Knowledge acquisition:* Identify missing information and make a plan to find it and integrate into the project. *Knowledge co-creation:* Generate new empirically-based factual knowledge from your collaborative project.
Conceptual knowledge	Dialogue to discuss relationships between ideas and recommendations generated by collaborative partners. Use synergistic collaboration to synthesise and meld complex ideas.	*Knowledge exchange:* Share perspectives and experiences. *Knowledge transfer:* Coach or guide collaborative partners to access and use conceptual knowledge in new project. *Knowledge acquisition:* Identify missing theoretical and conceptual knowledge and make a plan to find it and integrate into the project. *Knowledge co-creation:* Generate new concepts from your collaborative project.

(Continued)

Table 5.2 Continued

Knowledge domain	Taxonomy of Collaboration	Knowledge learning
Procedural knowledge	Dialogue to determine procedures the group will use to complete the project.	*Knowledge exchange:* Share practical experiences with conducting research, writing, publishing, presenting, or other activities collaborative partners need to complete the project. *Knowledge transfer:* Coach or guide collaborative partners in procedures beneficial to the project. *Knowledge acquisition:* Identify missing steps in designing, planning, and conducting the project, and make a plan to find how-to information as needed. *Knowledge co-creation:* Document successful procedures your collaborative partners used to complete the project.
Metacognitive knowledge	Reflect on your role and contributions to the project, and make sense of your experience as part of a collaboration.	*Knowledge exchange:* Share facts and background research important to the project. *Knowledge transfer:* Coach or guide collaborative partners to access and use foundational knowledge in new project. *Knowledge acquisition:* Identify missing information and make a plan to find it and integrate into the project. *Knowledge co-creation:* Reflect on your project and connect it to larger purposes and impact on the field or society at large.

employee, or faculty member, you have a lot to learn. In some situations, you may be paired with a mentor or a buddy, at least until you get settled. In other situations, you might feel that you are expected to navigate the new world on your own. In either case, for the people with whom you can learn from and with, in order to succeed in your new role.

What could go wrong?

As a new instructor or postdoc you could encounter resistance from experienced faculty, who are reluctant to accept you as an equal partner. You might feel that others are unwilling to discuss and agree to a shared purpose for your work together. Your suggestions could be interpreted as disrespectful of their efforts, which may have been honed over time. For some faculty in traditional academic settings 'shared purpose' might seem like a denigration of the purpose that has guided them before you came into the group.

If you are co-teaching or teaching sections of the same course with partners higher in the academic hierarchy you might find they are less likely to negotiate ownership of the syllabus or make changes (Morelock et al., 2017). In such situations, you will need to show respect for approaches currently in use, before recommending revisions or changes. Volunteer to take on parts of the project that others see as tedious, build credibility as a team player willing to do whatever is needed. Ask for clear boundaries and define where you can be flexible in your own instructional delivery, and where you must work within existing boundaries. Once the experienced faculty see what you can do within their frameworks, they will trust that your innovative ideas will not be damaging to their reputations and be more welcoming.

You could also encounter resistance from students who have negative attitudes based on prior experiences with poorly-managed group work. In this case as well, credibility is key. Let students know that you will assess work fairly, and recognise individual as well as group efforts. Evaluation of their work, including peer assessments, should reflect not only the final product but also the collaborative learning (Lee, Kim, & Byun, 2017).

Take it away

When people collaborate, they think together as well as work together. Such activities provide opportunities for people to learn from each other or transfer knowledge. Together they can acquire new skills or generate innovative new ideas, or new applications for best practices. Collaborative, cooperative, team, peer, and other styles of social learning are not new—but with the advent of diverse forms of electronic communications, the ways social learning occurs are continually evolving.

Try it! Exercises and questions for discussion and reflection

Individual reflection:

- When I have experienced successful learning from or with others, what roles did instructors or leaders play? Can I develop those approaches?

- What strengths do I bring to any roles I take as instructor or teaching assistant in terms of knowledge domains and the collaborative process?
- What will students need in order to trust me as their instructor, and each other as collaborative partners?
- What will students need in order to trust that any reflective writing, such as journals, will not be shared without their knowledge and agreement?

Group reflection

What will students need in order to trust that any agreements made by the group will be honoured by all collaborative partners? These might include confidentiality or ways to handle sensitive information.

Exercise

Review this sample assignment, with options for different styles of completion. Develop a sample assignment in your own field or discipline that follows this example. Use the collaborative work design styles described in the Taxonomy of Collaboration (Salmons, 2019).

Time to complete the assignment, curricular goals and learning objectives, availability of groupware, shared online folders or other tools, degree of trust and characteristics of the students are among the factors to be considered.

The United Nations Global Education Monitoring released the 2019 Report: *Migration, Displacement & Education: Building Bridges, Not Walls* (download: https://en.unesco.org/gem-report/report/2019/migration). The class or group is divided into dyads, and each dyad must develop a written analysis of key points from the chapters they select.

Parallel work design

After meeting to discuss the report as a whole, they decide to divide it up evenly. Each student selects chapters of the report to review. Each summarises the findings, trends, and key issues of the chapter and posts in the online classroom or a shared folder. After reviewing each other's work, they compile the reviews into one document and submit.

Sequential work design

After meeting to discuss the report as a whole, they decide to organise a step-by-step review process. After studying chapters 1–3 of the report, the first learner explains trends in internal and international migration, as well as key educational challenges. Building on the trends identified by Learner 1, Learner 2 reviews chapters 4–6 and discusses issues of diversity and displacement related to internal and international migration. Building on the trends and issues identified by Students 1 and 2, Learner 3 looks at implications for teachers and educational facilities described in the report. Learner 4 compiles an initial draft and organises a meeting to discuss completion of the written report.

Synergistic work design

After reviewing the report individually and making note of problems and policy recommendations, the group brainstorms possible strategies for addressing problems raised in the report. They discuss pros and cons of each, then make a decision about which to recommend. They schedule a time to work together to compile and edit their notes and generate the report.

Compare and contrast strategies

After all dyads create their reports, they exchange and review. The project concludes with a discussion of the pros and cons of each work design.

References

Anderson, L., Bloom, B. S., Krathwohl, D., & Airasian, P. (2000). *Taxonomy for learning, teaching and assessing: A revision of Bloom's Taxonomy of Educational Objectives* (2nd ed.). New York: Allyn & Bacon, Inc.

Bloom, B., Engelhart, M., Furst, E., Hill, W., & Krathwohl, D. (1956). *Taxonomy of educational objectives: Book 1, Cognitive domain*. New York: David McKay and Company.

Lee, H.-J., Kim, H., & Byun, H. (2017). Are high achievers successful in collaborative learning? An explorative study of college students' learning approaches in team project-based learning. *Innovations in Education & Teaching International*, *54*(5), 418–427. doi:10.1080/14703297.2015.1105754

Morelock, J. R., Lester, M. M., Klopfer, M. D., Jardon, A. M., Mullins, R. D., Nicholas, E. L., & Alfaydi, A. S. (2017). Power, perceptions, and relationships: A model of co-teaching in higher education. *College Teaching*, *65*(4), 182–191. doi:10.1080/87567555.2017.1336610

Salmons, J. (2019). *Learning to collaborate, collaborating to learn: Engaging students in the classroom and online*. Sterling: Stylus.

6 Collaboration and co-research

What will you learn by studying this chapter?

Chapter 6 focuses on ways to approach research collaborations as doctoral student, early career researcher, or new faculty member. For some students, the research experiences in Masters and doctoral programmes were largely individual. Students from these highly individualised programmes can find the transition to collaborative research somewhat intimidating. Others may have had collaborative experiences on student research teams where roles and expectations were clearly defined by faculty members who were the principal investigators. Students with this kind of background confined the transition to collegial research collaborations somewhat disorienting. In this chapter you will study and reflect on ways to build on your strengths and prepare for your role as collaborative researchers.

The strategies discussed in Chapter 6, particularly with regard to organising the collaborative process and communicating with partners, also apply to collaborative writing, discussed in Chapter 7. Similarly, strategies discussed in Chapter 7 can also be pertinent in collaborative research projects.

In this chapter you will gain an understanding of:

- How to identify ways the principles introduced throughout this book can be applied in a research setting.
- How to evaluate strategies for conducting research collaboratively.
- How to analyse options for using technology in the dispersed research project.
- How to compare and contrast approaches for overcoming collaborative inertia.

The big picture: Collaboration in a research setting

Some say that the era of the lone researcher has passed, and that to build credibility researchers need to work collaboratively (Cheek, 2008). Jeanes et al. point out several reasons why researchers are compelled to collaborate, whether they want to or not:

- to address complex research problems,
- institutional pressures,
- meet funding requirements, or
- to meet performance indicators. (Jeanes, Loacker & Śliwa, 2014, pp. 41–42)

Proctor and Vu observed: 'Collaboration among researchers with different expertise can potentially lead to novel solutions to the problems and to new discoveries, inventions, and interventions that would not be achieved otherwise' (Proctor & Vu, 2019). How should we move forward in this critical, potentially career-changing part of our academic lives? Let's begin by revisiting some of the ideas and principles introduced in earlier chapters of this book:

- Collaborative experiences common to students, early career researchers, and faculty members can include situations where individuals choose who to work with on what project, and situations where you participate, but have little choice in the strategic direction of the project (Chapters 1 and 3).
- When collaboration is complex and involves a number of factors such as cultural or disciplinary differences, or geographic dispersion of the group across time zones, it is unrealistic to expect that it can proceed without taking the time to think through goals and plan how the group will communicate and work together (Chapter 1).
- Collaboration allows for the utilisation of strengths and skills to support individual and collective flourishing (Chapters 2 and 4).
- Collaborative advantage is the term used for efforts that successfully engage partners in achieving something together, and collaborative inertia is the term used to describe the forces that work against successful collaboration.
- Collaborative learning is often central to collaborative projects because we need to learn new approaches and procedures to conduct research (Chapter 4).
- Self-care is important so we can function responsibly with collaborative partners (Chapter 3).

We need all of these ways of thinking and preparing when we conduct research collaboratively.

The nature of collaborative research

Why conduct research collaboratively? Leadbeater (2009) conceived of a degree of research innovation that is possible when we go beyond the collective gathering of information, beyond active construction of knowledge through dialogue, to ideas of knowledge creation through collaborative innovation. He suggests that the interpretative dimension of research can be highly collaborative, a cumulative and social activity in which people with different viewpoints, different skills, different insights share and develop ideas together (Leadbeater, 2009). This way of thinking echoes the modes of learning discussed in Chapter 5, where we looked at the *Collaborative Knowledge Learning Model*.

Let's reframe this model in a research context. Let's look at Figure 6.1, *Knowledge exchange*, which describes a level of collaboration that occurs when given we share

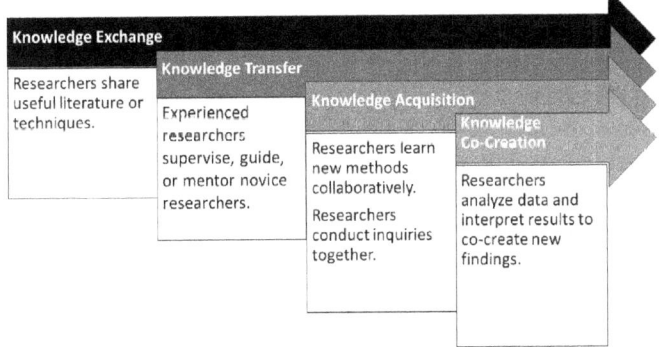

Figure 6.1 Collaborative knowledge learning in a research context.

information or resources with another researcher. Knowledge exchange could occur when researchers share relevant literature, or when they share information that will help the other conduct the study, such as access to research sites for participants. *Knowledge transfer* describes a level of collaboration that occurs we learn from an experienced research partner by sharing our expertise or knowledge. Knowledge transfer could take place when, for example, one partner is an expert in using specific data analysis software that other partners have not used. The experienced partner transfers that knowledge to the others for the benefit of the project as a whole. *Knowledge acquisition* describes learning that takes place when partners acquire new skills or knowledge that they did not have prior to the collaboration. Knowledge acquisition is at the heart of almost every research project because we learn something new when we answer research questions or prove the hypotheses. *Knowledge co-creation*, by contrast, refers to the collaborative generation of new knowledge, solutions, or practices. When we move into the level of collaborative interpretation and make new meanings from research findings, we co-create new knowledge.

Inherent in these definitions is the opportunity for a more experienced researcher to mentor and assist a less experienced one or for a more confident researcher to encourage and include a less confident one (Hafernik, Messerschmitt, & Vandrick, 1997). Vygotsky, an early educational theorist and a pioneer of social learning, described any person who possesses a higher skill level as a *more knowledgeable other*. Using the above Collaborative Knowledge Learning Model, we could say that sometimes peers are the knowledgeable others. Or, we might need to seek knowledgeable others from outside of our classroom or research team. As partners in a collaborative research project we might occasionally *be* the knowledgeable other, and still *need* a knowledgeable other willing to transfer skills important to success of the study.

Young and Pérez (2011) observe that collaborative innovation challenges the traditional assumptions, values, and practices of knowledge creation as an individual pursuit (p. 8). As a new and emerging scholar, you might find your roles in collaborative research could be constrained to a narrow role in data collection or data analysis; alternatively, you might have free rein to co-design a study and work collaboratively through all stages of the process. Aim for innovation and quality contribution, regardless of how responsible or lowly your position might be in the research group. By understanding both the potential for collaborative research and the elements that go into it, you will be prepared when you have the opportunity to take a leadership role.

Collaborative research across disciplines

As a Masters then a doctoral student, you most likely studied within a particular discipline, such as business, education, or sociology. Think about curricular programmes offered in your college and university that are hybrids of multiple fields, such as bioethics, or gender studies. How did these new fields emerge?

When you begin to research collaboratively in your professional or academic career, you can expect to move beyond your own discipline. As emphasised by the US National Academy of Sciences, collaboration is essential to 'advance fundamental understanding or to solve problems whose solutions are beyond the scope of a single discipline or field of research practice' (Andreasen & Brown, 2005, p. 26). This can be challenging, and even disorienting, when you discover that others do not share the norms, and even the language, that you are accustomed to using. Ways of thinking, epistemologies, and even methodologies can vary greatly across academic disciplines. For example, in some disciplines researchers conduct research and publish studies that use qualitative, quantitative, and mixed methods. In other disciplines, quantitative research methods are used almost exclusively.

Levels of disciplinarity

Let us differentiate between levels of disciplinary collaboration (Andreasen & Brown, 2005; J. E. Salmons & Wilson, 2009) (see Figure 6.2. Crossing disciplinary boundaries):

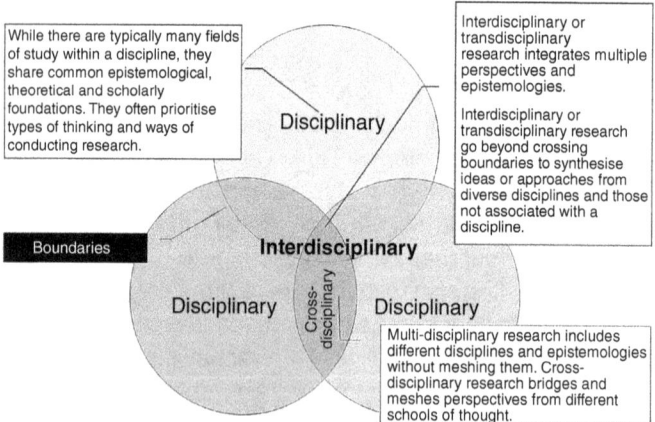

Figure 6.2 Crossing disciplinary boundaries.

- **Multi-disciplinary:** Researchers make use of more than one discipline. They work in parallel or sequentially from disciplinary-specific base to address a common problem. While researchers draw on more than one discipline, they do not mesh ideas from those disciplines.
- **Cross-disciplinary:** Researchers coordinate efforts by involving two or more disciplines. Researchers look for ways to bridge different schools of thought to address a common problem.
- **Interdisciplinary:** Researchers work jointly and integrate concepts, frameworks, or approaches from two or more disciplines to address a common problem.
- **Transdisciplinary:** Researchers work jointly, developing and using a new shared conceptual framework drawing together disciplinary-specific theories, concepts, and approaches to address a common problem. Transdisciplinary thinking transcends boundaries of conventional disciplines.

As you can see from the progression illustrated in these definitions, the defining characteristics of disciplinarity are not about how many disciplines are present in the group, but, more importantly, the degree to which disciplinary knowledge will be incorporated. The US National Academy of Sciences notes the importance of integration of information, data, techniques, tools, perspectives, concepts, and/or theories from two or more disciplines or bodies of specialised knowledge. They affirm 'It is not just pasting two disciplines together to create one product but rather is an integration and synthesis of ideas and methods' (Andreasen & Brown, 2005, p. 26).

For example, let's say an education researcher and a business researcher are both interested in leadership. If they are on a committee together at their university, they would be part of a *multidisciplinary* project. If the education researcher started using articles from the business researcher's syllabus, and comparing and applying theories developed by business scholars, they could say the course is *cross-disciplinary*. The education researcher and business researcher could conduct an *interdisciplinary* study of management education. The education researcher and business researcher could develop a new *transdisciplinary* model for leadership in any setting.

When we look at a potential problem to investigate, it is important to think through whether the study should be conducted collaboratively, and what other disciplines are needed to be a part of the study, at what stage? Then, we need to think about how deeply we want to engage these representatives in the research. Is it enough to bring experts from different disciplines together, perhaps to gain new insights into a potential research problem? Or will the resolution of that problem require us to meld thinking and perspectives? Can we, for example, discover solutions to persistent problems like poverty by studying them solely from an economic angle, or do we need to understand social, psychological, political, historical, and other influences?

How do you move forward when collaborating with researchers, community members, and other stakeholders to represent other disciplines? Collaborative research that crosses disciplines means we are crossing the kinds of boundaries discussed in Chapter 1. Proctor and Vu know just how hard that can be:

> A researcher goes through years of intense training and education to become highly skilled in one discipline, making it difficult for that individual to become skilled in other disciplines. With multidisciplinary team research, one does not have to master multiple disciplines but needs to be able to understand the contributions of other

> disciplines and to communicate with experts from those disciplines.
>
> (Proctor & Vu, 2019, p. 271)

First, keep an open mind. Be mindful of your own biases and preferences. Reflect on your standards and expectations for what constitutes research ethics and research quality. Are there some are there some areas where you simply can't negotiate?

To understand others' contributions, listen and reflect on what you hear before disagreeing with perspectives that are unfamiliar or in conflict with your own academic background. The reason you are working together is grounded in a common purpose and the reason you have members from different disciplines is rooted in the need to look at the problem from a multiplicity of perspectives. As noted in Chapter 1, the more complexity and diversity present in the project, the greater the degree of care, agreement, and planning is required in preparation. As a basic rule of thumb, assume that the greater the differentiation between collaborative partners, the more time will be needed to plan and prepare. It is important for each collaborative partner to think from the outset about their closely held ideas about research approaches, in order to avoid the confusion or discord that derail a collaborative project.

Use communication and technology: Collaboration tools

If we collaborate with people in our same locality or institution, we can readily find time for formal meetings or informal cups of coffee. We can easily share any documents or artefacts associated with the research project. We can look on the department calendar to find out which of our colleagues are busy with other commitments or are out of town. However, more often, we will be working with people who are not in the immediate vicinity. Indeed, we might find ourselves in collaborations with partners we have never met face-to-face.

Software and electronic communication tools allow partners to build the relationships, and undertake the tasks, needed to work collaboratively. We might discover that we are more efficient working electronically. Or we might find that working online introduces even more inertia that can delay the project, and overwhelm or alienate partners. To work collaboratively at a distance, we need to be intentional and strategic.

Systems, software, and access

Before we can decide whether we are on the same page, we need to decide what 'page' we will use. Here are a few questions you will want to review with your collaborative partners:

- Do we have access to the same, or compatible, tools and systems? Can we find free or open source tools that all of us can use? If not, are there cost or skill factors we will need to consider? Who will be responsible for setting up and managing software or accounts? Who will make sure everyone has working passwords to group files, without allowing such files to be jeopardised by unauthorised access?

If we are meeting by telephone, voice-over-internet, or web conference tool:

- Do all partners have access to toll-free conference lines for telephone? Alternatively, do all partners have headsets for voice-over-Internet calls? If web conferencing will be used, do all partners have the ability to use and view shared screens and annotation tools? Will calls be recorded? Will such recordings be archived for future reference? How will private calls or calls about sensitive information be protected? Who will facilitate the call(s)?

Shared files, folders, and calendars

One way that collaborative partners work together, whether they are co-located or dispersed, is through the use of shared online files. Free and inexpensive digital tools are available that can be used even when researchers are on a tight budget.

Popular commercial options include Dropbox, Box, and Google Drive, which offer both free and paid levels, depending on the amount of storage needed. Dropbox works with any type of file. Google Drive allows you to use their own open access word-processing and spreadsheet software, which could be helpful if some partners do not have access to Microsoft Office. Google Drive can be set up to align with a Google calendar, where due dates and meeting times are available for all to see, and automatic reminders can be set.

Make sure that all partners have access to the shared files, folders, and calendars and know how to use them. Also make sure that it is someone's job to organise shared folders and keep everything, including the calendar, up to date.

Version control

The term *version control* simply means that we keep track of iterations of a document, and have the ability to return to a previous instance of the work. Version control is, however, easier said than done when we have a group of people trying to work on one document! Version control is an important part of the task when it comes to collaborative projects. At the most basic level, develop a system and naming protocol from the outset of the project, to avoid confusion.

Wikis

Wikis allow you go a step beyond shared folders and also include spaces for chats, comments, scheduling and calendars, and communications. In other words, these platforms allow collaborative partners to keep many parts of the project in one place, which allows for overall coherence and ease of coordination. Wikis are defined as:

> A website or database developed collaboratively by a community of users, allowing any user to add and edit content.
>
> (*Wiki*, 2019)

Popular commercial options, such as MediaWiki, Wikidot, and PbWorks, include both free and subscription portals. Slack, a team messaging platform, includes many of the user-sharing features of a wiki.

Young and Pérez described the use of a wiki in an international research collaboration in the music education field (Young & Pérez, 2011). They present two main benefits the use of the wiki can bring to research: to enable the integration and navigation across and between media of different forms and to promote research as a collective and social rather than an individual practice (p. 4). They observe that:

> The significance of using a wiki, and the ideals of collaborative research that it represents, is that it makes sharing central to the dynamism of intellectual, academic production that has hitherto, been built on individual ownership of ideas in the form of property. (p. 8)

Lessons from their reflections on collaborative research can be helpful to others who want to share data in the forms of images, audio files, or multi-media, as well as text-based files and drafts. Perhaps we can learn from their experience.

In the study conducted by Young, Pérez and others, data collection involved videos, which would be large and unwieldy to share by email. Because their videos featured children and families whose identities needed to be shielded from public disclosure, a password-protected wiki was ideal for the project. Young and Pérez (2011) note that:

> Photos, written commentaries, sections of interview data and video clips can be chunked, selected, copied, pasted, juxtaposed and compared to allow for similarities and patterns to emerge leading to themes and interpretations… hyperlinks with other sites containing relevant information can be included when and where appropriate, and theoretical material (mainly articles) that informs certain emerging interpretations can be uploaded. (pp. 8–9)

When you are approaching a collaborative project, think about the types and scale of data you plan to collect, and the types of interaction you will need to develop with co-researchers. Are shared folders adequate, or might you need a more robust platform such as a wiki?

Inertia and technology

Technology can help us come together… or not. Electronic communication can help us get things done or become an obstacle. Hoffman and research team (2014) conducted an ethnography of their own process, with a focus on technology. They identified some points, as noted in the annotations, that we could call collaborative inertia in that they distracted collaborative partners from the substance of their work and obstructed the overall project. Let's look at what they found and think through ways of overcoming the problems.

One participant observed:

> … at first, I was an advocate of the online tools, but soon I felt inundated … I was getting a lot of information (1), the vast majority was not priority or interesting (2). The other problem was that I often wanted to reply to some comment, but couldn't find it. The time that I was losing trying to find things (3) led me to quit [the collaborative platform] and concentrate on good old, reliable e-mail! In this project, e-mail and Skype were the two critical tools. The other ICT tools enabled much greater interaction with the CRP members, but, in terms of social engagement and trust building, nothing can replace face to face meetings and events (4).
>
> (Hoffman et al., 2014, p. 484)

We can interpret this thoughtful comment and add tips for better collaborative practice:

- Avoid information overload.
- Agree to protocols for how you will discern what needs to be shared, or simply filed so that others can use it when needed.
- Develop and use protocols to tag emails and posts to wikis or other shared sites. For example, label a message 'action needed,' or 'for your files' so your partners can proceed accordingly.
- Create a simple, but manageable system for organising messages or documents so partners do not become overwhelmed and frustrated when they can't find what they need. Use the fewest, simplest tools necessary to accomplish the tasks. If you have a choice between a robust platform that includes messaging, calendaring, version control and file storage versus using separate software for each one, choose the integrated option. If email and Skype are all you need, then stick with the tools you know.

Cases and examples

Let's connect with our case studies to support your thinking:

Phillipe is working on his doctoral research. While he is responsible for conducting the study on his own, he views his approach as a collaboration to the degree that it involves reciprocal cooperation with gatekeepers at the research site. As Phillipe navigates his doctoral work and his teaching commitments within the Faculty he utilises digital platforms to communicate with his supervisors and a project where roles involve others with which he is engaging. He has focused on utilising the university's calendar to give him an insight into his peers' available time, and when he finds it defunct to find a common time for a meeting he has used the online platform doodle poll (https://doodle.com/en/) to suggest possible meeting dates and times to work with others to find a time that will work for all.

Alicia's postdoc is centred on a longitudinal research project. While she shares responsibilities with others on the research team, she does not view their relationship as *collaborative*. The lead researchers have been collecting data for several years, so they are now unwilling to make changes. She is trying to learn as much as she can about conducting research on this scale. Alicia reflects on her work in daily journal entries. A part of this navigation is to book in meetings with team members to discuss how the data are being used and applied to specific contexts. This is to embrace learning from each other with a mutual respect. As she navigates this she has been able to work with the team leader to set up regular meet ups that involve fortnightly face-to-face informal meetings where each research team member shares what they are working on so that all partners can have an overview and be able to support one another while also being aware of project outcomes.

Collaboration and co-research 141

Jesse has been assigned one large introductory course and one seminar. The course is currently lecture-based, and the seminar is discussion-oriented. The field of study is one that leads to a team-based work life. They plan to revise both the seminar and course after the first year to include more collaborative projects that prepare students for professional success. They hope to work collaboratively with more experienced faculty on the updates. For now, they are studying team formation and leadership so they can contribute current thinking and engaging readings to the curriculum work group responsible for approving course and seminar revisions. As a part of this process discussions have been centred around the strength of appreciation for learning to utilise partner strengths in working face-to-face and online as they move forward with the shared goal.

Elizabeth is engaged in a research project at the NGO where she now works, with data collection underway at several agency sites. It is collaborative in that the researchers are working towards a shared goal larger than they could achieve on her own, but Elizabeth feels the parallel nature of the research in practice is not adequate. She would like to see more opportunities for synergistic interactions with the research team. The team agrees to utilise the Google Docs digital platform and introduce this as a way to enable the partners to share knowledge and approaches.

Into practice: Strategies to overcome the inertia that can sabotage collaborative research

Imagine being part of a team of researchers where no one has read the texts you think are fundamental to your way of thinking. They don't read the same journals. They don't understand your acronyms. You must spend longer in meetings to make sure everyone has a common understanding of next steps. Which of these perspectives will reflect your views after you have been a part of a collaborative research project?

Any researcher who has researched collaboratively, in whatever form, will attest to the

> ... tensions created by trying to work out how to pool resources, what resources to pool, and what disciplines and players to invite to work collaboratively, and how.
> (Cheek, 2008, p. 1599)

Or

> Researching and writing with colleagues can be very productive and enjoyable in ways that single researching and authoring may not necessarily be. We have found that collaborating on research and writing projects has enriched our personal and professional lives and has helped us make contributions to our institution, profession, and community.
> (Hafernik et al., 1997, pp. 33, 37)

Collaboration can be difficult, and research is possibly one of the more difficult contexts for collaborative work.

As scholars, we are driven by the questions we want to ask and tenure or promotion may rely on the quality of the work we produce. The characteristics that Huxham identified as collaborative inertia can be magnified when the stakes are high (Huxham & Vangen, 2004, 2005). At the same time, research projects are typically large and require a lot of work. If we can share the effort with others, we can get more done. We can turn to someone else for help if we run into a snag, or need to take a few days off because we're sick. We can avoid the solitary slog and share everyday trials and frustrations.

After working with contributors to a special issue on multidisciplinary collaboration, Proctor and Vu (2019) identified some best practices that can help you deal with the challenges. They point to the importance of having good leadership that sets the tone and direction for achieving specific outcomes. Hanganu-Opatz et al., writing advice to new faculty members, emphasised the importance of mentoring your team members professionally and personally (Hanganu-Opatz, Mameli, Káradóttir, & Spires-Jones, 2015). As a new researcher, possibly a member of a larger project, you might not have the opportunity to serve as a leader right now. However, you can observe exemplary leadership styles. Contrast how some leaders mentor others, and encourage them to learn and work together to co-create new knowledge, whereas some leaders who do not. Work to develop those positive leadership capacities.

Proctor and Vu (2019) emphasised that 'in addition to formal communication, informal interactions provide opportunities for individuals to get to know each other better' (p. 275). When the collaboration occurs primarily through electronic communications, intentional efforts are needed to allow collaborative partners to get acquainted. Getting to know each other as human beings, not only as producers of written documents, is important in any collaboration, but essential when the project is complex and sensitive. Take the time to encourage an inclusive, fun laboratory or research environment to foster enthusiasm for the project (Hanganu-Opatz et al., 2015). And don't forget to celebrate success!

What could go wrong?

Research is a challenging process that typically spans a significant time frame. Even the most collegial working group can run into problems at one stage or another. Lingard et al. (2007), in a discussion of their reflections on collaborative research, observed that 'research processes must acknowledge and work through these tensions, because when handled well they can lead to analytic insights, but handled poorly they can undermine team coherence', (p. 515).

Whether you enter collaborative research from the beginning and can shape the purpose and plans, or enter when the project is underway, strive to answer fundamental questions, importantly:

- Plan thoroughly and agree to who does what, when. Set checkpoints for the project;
- Know your strengths and the situations that make you uncomfortable in collaborative projects;
- Be willing to initiate difficult conversations, but use synchronous communications to avoid unintended interpretations of your messages; and
- Assess contributions of each partner, and credit their work accordingly.

The proactive and positive strategies recommended throughout this book are especially relevant in research partnerships.

Take it away

Chapter 6 offered an overview of some key ideas for collaborative researchers. Understanding how and why our work together is significant, and our position in relation to partners can help us to prepare for collaborative research projects. When we are self-aware about our strengths and weaknesses we can identify when we will need knowledge exchange, or transfer with a more knowledgeable other, and when we can take the lead and mentor less experienced partners. By realising the different ways we can work across disciplines, we can take advantage of opportunities for research projects that will come in a variety of perspectives. On the practical side, in today's connected world we find that using electronic communications can help us work efficiently and build relationships with collaborative partners near and far.

Try it: Exercises and questions for discussion and reflection

Individual reflection:
  Look at Figure 6.3 and consider:

- What boundaries would be easy for you to cross? Why?
- What boundaries would be difficult for you to cross? Why?
- What boundaries would you refuse to cross? Why?

146 *Collaboration and co-research*

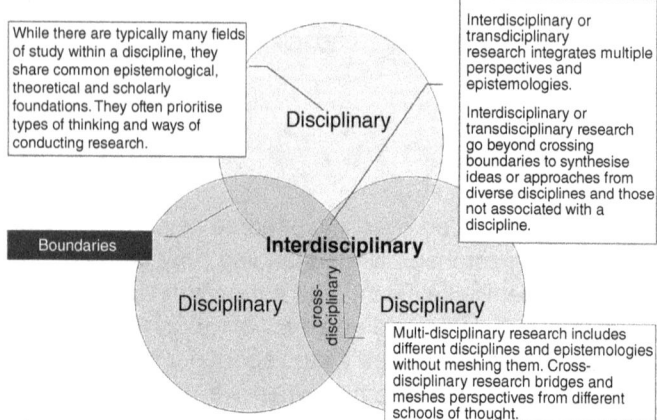

Figure 6.3 Boundary exercise.

Group exercise:

Working in small groups, select a current topic of interest. Look for articles that represent multi-, cross-, inter-, and transdisciplinary approaches. Compare and contrast them in your discussion. Identify, as possible, the styles of collaboration used by the writers of these articles.

References

Andreasen, N. C., & Brown, T. L. (2005). *Facilitating interdisciplinary research*. Retrieved from Washington, D.C.: https://www.nap.edu/read/11153

Cheek, J. (2008). Researching collaboratively: Implications for qualitative research and researchers. *Qualitative Health Research*, *18*(11), 1599–1603. doi:10.1177/1049732308324865

Hafernik, J. J., Messerschmitt, D. S., & Vandrick, S. (1997). Research news and comment: Collaborative research why and how? *Educational Researcher*, *26*(9), 31–35. doi:10.3102/0013189X026009031

Hanganu-Opatz, I. L., Mameli, M., Káradóttir, R. T., & Spires-Jones, T. L. (2015). You are not alone: selecting your group members and leading an outstanding research team. *European Journal of Neuroscience*, *42*(12), 3012–3017. doi:10.1111/ejn.13109

Hoffman, D., Blasi, B., Ćulum, B., Dragšić, Ž., Ewen, A., Horta, H., Nokkala, T., & Rios-Aguilar, C. (2014). The methodological illumination of a blind spot: information and communication technology and international research team dynamics in a higher education research program. *Higher Education*, *67*(4), 473–495. doi:10.1007/s10734-013-9692-y

Huxham, C., & Vangen, S. (2005). *Managing to collaborate: The theory and practice of collaborative advantage*. Oxford: Routledge.

Huxham, C., & Vangen, S. I. V. (2004). Realizing the advantage or Succumbing to inertia? *Organizational Dynamics*, *33*(2), 190–201. https://doi.org/10.1016/j.orgdyn.2004.01.006

Jeanes, E., Loacker, B., & Śliwa, M. (2014). Researcher collaboration: learning from experience. In E. Jeanes & T. Huzzard (Eds.), *Critical management research: Reflections from the field*. London: SAGE Publications Ltd. Retrieved from https://methods.sagepub.com/book/critical-management-research. doi:10.4135/9781446288610

Leadbeater, C. W. (2009). *We-think: Mass innovation, not mass production: The power of mass creativity*. London: Proile Books Ltd.

Lingard, L., Schryer, C. F., Spafford, M. M., & Campbell, S. L. (2007). Negotiating the politics of identity in an interdisciplinary research team. *Qualitative Research*, *7*(4), 501–519. doi:10.1177/1468794107082305

Proctor, R. W., & Vu, K.-P. L. (2019). How psychologists help solve real-world problems in multidisciplinary research teams: introduction to the special issue. *American Psychologist*, *74*(3), 271–277. doi:10.1037/amp0000458

Salmons, J. E., & Wilson, L. A. (2009). Online collaborative integration and recommendations for future research. In J. E. Salmons & L. A. Wilson (Eds.), *Handbook of research on electronic collaboration and organizational synergy* (Vol. *II*). Hershey: Information Science Reference.

Wiki. (2019). Oxford: Oxford Press.

Young, S., & Pérez, J. (2011). 'We-research': Adopting a wiki to support the processes of collaborative research among a team of international researchers. *International Journal of Music Education*, *30*(1), 3–17. doi:10.1177/0255761411410144

7 Collaborative writing

What will you learn by studying this chapter?

This chapter introduces collaboration in the context of writing and publishing. We will explore co-authoring roles and expectations. We will think about ways the writing project might cross disciplinary boundaries. Using the Taxonomy of Collaboration, we'll think about ways to plan and map collaborative projects using different types of work designs. We will build on the strategies described in Chapter 6, particularly those related to communication and technology, since they also apply when we are engaged in collaborative writing projects.

In this chapter you will gain an understanding of:

- How to plan and carry out collaborative writing and publishing projects.
- How to develop agreements about content and protocols for voice, format, and style.
- How to address common dilemmas.
- How to work with external players (editors, reviewers, other contributors).

The big picture: What is collaborative writing?

Writing a book or an article is a demanding process in the best of circumstances. We must balance a number of internal and external factors. We must figure out how to convey our insights and experiences, research and analysis, in writing. At the same time, we must interface with the external world: schedules and deadlines, editors and publishers, and, ultimately, with our readers. We add another set of factors when we work with co-authors on articles, books, or edited collections, or on practical materials such as grant proposals or reports.

We want to take a positive view here, but we need to be realistic. There are common obstacles tied to inertia that can hamper successful collaboration. The sooner we identify them, the sooner we can address them (and avoid damage that will take time to repair). Obstacles can include:

- **Ambiguous purpose:** Are we here for the same reasons?
- **Leadership confusion:** How will we make decisions and coordinate efforts?
- **Trust issues:** Can I be sure you will fulfill your commitment to the collaboration?
- **Communication breakdown:** Is everyone present? Can we agree about how and when to communicate?
- **Technical issues:** Do technologies help or hinder the collaboration?

The more factors involved, the more cultural or disciplinary boundaries crossed, the more you need a systematic approach to collaborative writing! How can we navigate all of these dimensions in ways that allow us to collectively produce our best work?

Let's revisit our definition of collaboration:

> Collaboration is an interactive process that engages two or more partners who work together to achieve value and outcomes they could not accomplish independently.
>
> (Salmons, 2019, p. 5)

This definition suggests that the decision to collaborate should start with a purpose, with an understanding about how the value and outcomes for the proposed project are improved by the contributions from collaborative partners. The purpose of a writing project can come from internal or external sources. Sometimes we meet people we would like to work with and determine the topics we would like to create together. The purpose is clear and comes naturally as we discuss what is important to each of us. Other times we are assigned or required to contribute to a collaborative writing project with others we may or may not know. In such cases, external stakeholders have a role to play in determining the purpose, style, and form of the writing project. In these situations, we need to make time to be sure everyone has bought into a purpose generated externally.

Leadership and decision-making

The interactive writing process can be organised and coordinated in a variety of ways. It's important to think about who will do the organising and coordinating when you are embarking on a complex writing project, and how you will decide the best approaches to use. Are there decision-making styles with which all partners are familiar, or do you need to come up with your own process?

The matter of leadership is hard to avoid when multiple writers are engaged. Even when the collaboration involves a group of equals, leadership is needed. Thanks to leadership, communication takes place, meetings are scheduled, progress keeps moving forward, editors or stakeholders are kept in the loop, and the project is completed.

Leadership does not mean one person is the leader. You might decide to use different styles of leadership at different points of the project. There might be times when you want a top-down, just-tell-us-what-to-do approach, such as completion of a proposal or copy-editing the manuscript. And times you want shared leadership, such as when you are brainstorming new ideas or planning a presentation about your book to share at a conference. You might decide that one partner takes the lead on a specific aspect of the project, such as communicating with editors or publishers, and another takes the lead on editing final drafts. Here are a few questions to help you think through your options:

- **Internal or external leadership?** How much latitude does your group have to decide the approach they want to use? Are there external stakeholders, such as a provost or a funder, who must be consulted?
- **Individual or shared leadership?** Depending on the scale of the project and commitments of the partners, a team effort might be needed.
- **Fixed or rotating leadership?** Is there someone who has strengths in organisation and coordination who will take a lead role throughout? Or does it make sense to rotate the roles of project coordination.

As per our definition, the input of collaborative partners is needed to do something that the individuals could not do on their own. Among the reasons for writers to collaborate are:

- Desire for multiple perspectives, or multiple research foundations and interpretations of the topic,
- Expectation for less work by each partner by sharing the load, or
- Ability to reach readers who recognise the names of one or more authors.

Not every writing project is potentially improved by the input of co-authors. Sometimes we might prefer to complete the project on our own, and sometimes that is exactly what we will do. It is important to think through the nature of a project before deciding to approach it collaboratively. However, there are times when we have no choice. We might be reporting on a collaborative research project, or we might be assigned to work on a team that includes a written outcome. One way or the other, we need to be prepared to write collaboratively.

Individual and collective outcomes

Outcomes of a collaborative process can be either *individual*, meaning each partner creates their own writing, or *collective,* meaning the completed piece of writing represents everyone's contributions. In maps and diagrams that use the Taxonomy of Collaboration, a string of stars represents individual outcomes, while a single star represents a collective outcome (Figure 7.1).

In the Taxonomy of Collaboration, stars represent outcomes of the collaborative process

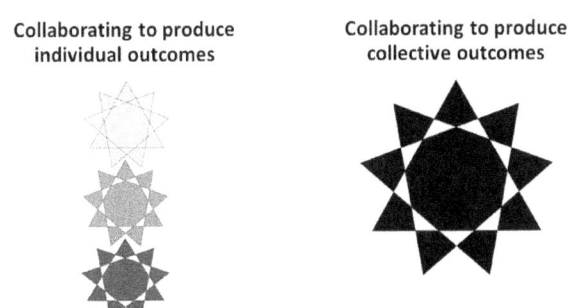

Figure 7.1 Individual and collective outcomes.

Writing groups and clubs whose members are working on individual projects abound inside and outside of academia. These writers collaborate to dialogue about their work and to offer reviews of work in progress. However, they complete their own dissertations, articles, or novels. We could simply map this kind of collaborative writing by using the Taxonomy of Collaboration (see Figure 7.2). The group begins (1) with a discussion to get acquainted, and to determine the roles, expectations, and parameters for critiques of each other's work. They each engage in mindful reflection throughout the process (2). They each go off to write on their own projects, knowing that they have the supportive group on hand if needed (3 and 5). Based on group agreements, they review each other's work and offer critiques (4). They arrange time for discussions as needed. Some writing groups read sections aloud and discuss them (6). With the encouragement and constructive suggestions of the group, members are able to complete their own piece of writing (7).

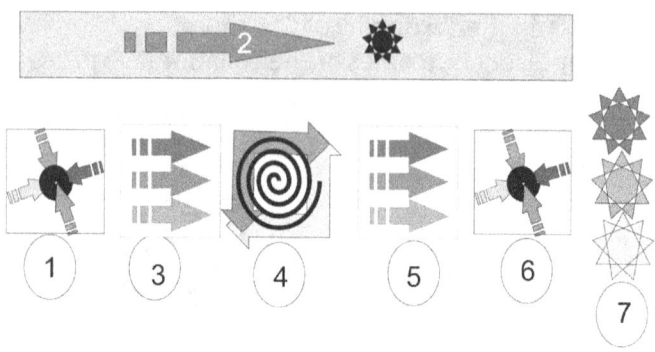

Figure 7.2 Mapping collaborative writing process, with individual outcomes.

Collaborative writing can also result in *collective outcomes*, such as when partners generate a written report or white paper, article, chapter, or book. The process of generating a piece of writing with one or more co-authors will typically entail individual writing along the way. Still, the effort of working together means each co-author must work with the goals, forms, and approaches of the group rather than prioritising their own style.

Cases and examples

 **Alicia** is feeling pressure to publish journal articles. She has a couple of drafts, but is not confident that she knows how to proceed. She met two other women in her field at a conference, and they decided to try writing together. One of the women has already published several articles. Alicia updated her literature review and

the others are happy to work with her to polish it into a publishable piece. They are now working in parallel, with one looking for the best journal for this submission, one working on the introduction, and one working on the discussion section. They have scheduled a time to meet face-to-face to pull this article together and plan the next one. Alicia is learning a lot about working remotely with other writers. They have created a system with shared folders that they can continue to use for future projects. Alicia feels good because her efforts to organise a thematic review for her dissertation have paid off. She appreciates the others' generosity, which makes her willing to help them on the next project.

Elizabeth did well on her thesis, and received many compliments from her university supervisors and committee members. However, she is not interested in writing in a purely academic style. She would like to develop a handbook or practical guide for others working in NGOs or agencies. It is a big project, so she would like to find partners. In the meantime, the NGO where she is working has assigned her to a team that is developing a substantive report for a major funder. She does not know the others on the team, but has an open mind about working with them. The funder has determined the criteria and format for the report, and their representative wants to give input along the way. She hopes that this project will give her the experience she needs to advance her own project.

Into practice: Why is it important to collaborate in writing and publishing?

Most co-authored projects will entail multiple stages over a period of time. A large project might combine more than one of these work designs. We might work primarily in parallel, with synergistic stages where we draft an introduction or craft the final conclusions together.

While the project is underway, the collaborative partners will undoubtedly have many other tasks, deadlines, and distractions. Careful planning is essential to success and will help partners prioritise their shared efforts. While small-scale collaborations can often proceed without a well-articulated plan, when more than three people are involved complications emerge. Making time to plan and agree to a collaborative process *before* we start the project can save precious hours in the long run. If you find yourself in a situation where pre-project planning was impossible, make an effort to step back and assess where you are and plan how to move forward.

Three important points should guide the planning stage, and we can use the Taxonomy of Collaboration to think about them:

1. **Agree to communicate**
   Communication and trust are interrelated: we develop mutual trust when we understand each other. To succeed in a high-stakes project such as collaborative writing we need to think carefully about how, and how often, to communicate. Will we set checkpoints and hold meetings on a regular basis or just connect on an as-needed basis? When

we send an email, what response time do we feel is appropriate? Who will be responsible for communicating with the editor, etc.?

Today much of the interactive process occurs electronically. Do we have access to the same digital tools and software? Will we use shared folders, or send drafts as email attachments? What form, format, and styles will we use for drafts? How will we manage versions as the project evolves?

2. **Design and agree on a work plan**
A work plan establishes who will do what, when, and how. In the Taxonomy of Collaboration, we see three ways to structure efforts completed by two or more people. With a *parallel* approach, we divide the project into component parts that are completed by individuals or small groups. A map might look similar to the one illustrated in Figure 7.2; in this case, however, we have a big difference. In Figure 7.3 we see that the outcome must integrate the partners' writing. This puts a lot more pressure on the discussion and review phases. In those

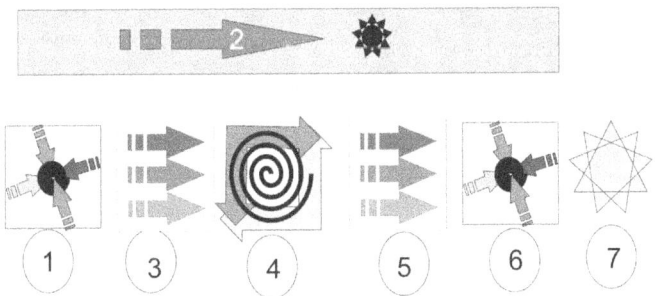

Figure 7.3 Collaborative writing with a parallel work design.

158　*Collaborative writing*

discussions, partners need to be very clear about the expectations for each member, and the criteria that will be used for review.

With a *sequential* approach, component parts are completed in a step-wise fashion. Individuals or small groups take responsibility for each step. For example, one partner might research competing texts and outline the market research section of the proposal, and another person might flesh out a description of the target market for the proposed book.

Our map is a little more complex in Figure 7.4. When we use a sequential design, we need to use the dialogue times (1 and 6), whether meetings or shared documents, to agree on how and when each stage will be completed, by whom. Characteristics and criteria, scheduling and timing, must be clear for each step so that the next collaborative partner(s) are able to build and move the project forward (3 and 5). At least one check-in or review stage (4) is important while the work is in progress. Partners who participated in earlier stages should have

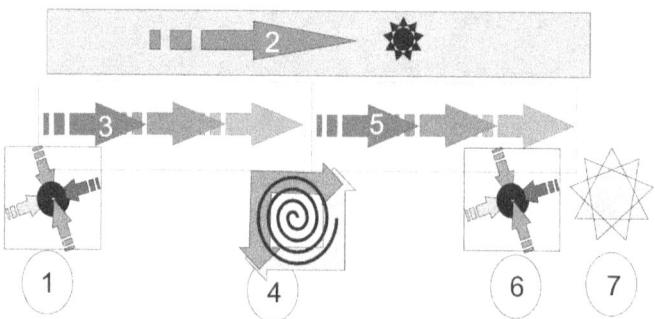

Figure 7.4 Collaborative writing with a sequential work design.

input at the final stages (6 and 7), even if their part of the project is complete (Figure 7.4).

With both parallel and sequential approaches, we will need to decide how to meld component parts into the final draft.

A third type of collaborative work design is *synergistic.* When we work synergistically, we do not divide the project into component parts, but instead brainstorm and work together to make decisions and create the project. We integrate 'meeting' and 'review' into the project; this is a holistic approach (1). Naturally, we still need to reflect on our own roles and perspectives on the project (2). See Figure 7.5.

One of these approaches is not any better than the other, but one might be more appropriate than another, given the people involved or the nature of the project. By knowing our own and our partners' strengths, we can allocate parts of the writing project and determine who is responsible for monitoring the process. Connecting to our

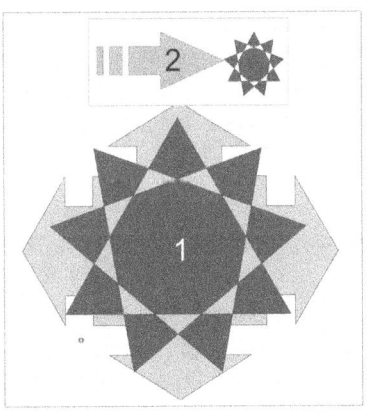

Figure 7.5 Collaborative writing with a synergistic work design.

strengths also provides a language to approach the collaborative writing process, including the decision on which journal, for example, or which audience you are to write for, approach to setting up the argument of the writing, how signposting for the reader will occur, or debating the wording of titles of heading. These are just some examples, however approaching them through your strengths and utilising your partners' different strengths offers one way to approach writing and making decisions. Refer back to Chapters 2 and 4 for specific strategies to approach working to your strengths.

3. **Use best practices for respectful participation**
   Collaborative writing calls on us to work at our best, even when we might disagree with others, or have a different perspective on the project. In Figure 7.6, see some suggested best practices associated with each dimension of the Taxonomy of Collaboration. And as you explore these approaches, in partnership with working with more experienced academics formally or informally, you can begin to 'gain practical and political "know how"' about the writing process and success in publication aligned to best practice (Kamler & Thomson, 2014, p. 163).

What could go wrong?

As doctoral and early career researchers, approaching collaborative writing is complex. As Kamler and Thomson (2014) remind us, 'writing culture does not simply happen. It must be consciously produced' (p. 159). We know collaborative is complex and dynamic, and this is often evident in

Collaborative writing 161

Taxonomy of Collaboration: Best Writing Practices

	MINDFUL REFLECTION • Use your journal or discussions with trusted friends to reflect on your collaborative writing experiences. • Make notes about your observations and experiences for future reference, when assessing the project or preparing for a new one.
	DIALOGUE • Communicate respectfully. • If disagreements or conflicts arise, use active listening and work towards positive resolution. Avoid personal attacks. • Participate actively in meetings with co-authors or co-editors. • Let partners know promptly when you have a problem or will miss a deadline. • Use shared folders or communication tools agreed upon by the group.
	REVIEW • Develop and follow review criteria. • Offer honest, constructive, formative feedback. • Provide timely responses.
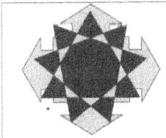	**PARALLEL COLLABORATION** • Follow agreed-upon formats, styles, voice. • Complete your part(s) of the project in a timely, complete, manner. • Alert partners to any issues or timing concerns.
	SEQUENTIAL COLLABORATION • Build on previous stages of the work; maintain styles and formats.. • Contact writer(s) from earlier stages if you have questions. • Complete your part(s) of the project in a timely, complete, manner.
	SYNERGISTIC COLLABORATION • Offer thoughtful, honest input to the group effort. • Listen to others. • Accept that not all of your ideas might be accepted into the collective work. <div align="right">c. Vision2Lead 2005-2020</div>

Arrow on right: Low Trust → High Trust

Figure 7.6 Best practices for collaborative writing.

the writing phase of your work as doctoral and early career researchers when engaging with co-authors. Aspects to this collaborative process can go wrong. So, let's have a look at some of these, remembering that suggestions in Chapter 4 which specifically address some behaviours that are common in collaboration are addressed there and can be transferred to the co-writing relationship, as well as connecting back to Chapter 2 and working with your strengths.

Idea flow issues

We are stuck with the formation of an idea or we have too many ideas in on paper and as co-authors we can't shift our thinking are common blockers when writing. One solution could be to utilise academic support services within your institution offered for writing advice. As a collaboration, seeking independent advice can offer another perspective, especially with the lens of another discipline to your own.

Feelings of isolation

Sometimes even when we are co-writing we can feel isolated during the process of writing. This can emerge for a number of reasons, and although this can feel like a hurdle that stop flow this can be interrupted with social support. Consider a writing group that can offer and foster the development of linguistic and academic literacies while also providing social support about the process. Writing groups are also a wonderful way to glean feedback. You could form a writing group as part of your collaboration or you could collaborate with other writers about the process of writing to support feelings of isolation.

Finding it hard to find time

Time management is crucial for any collaboration, and when writing dedicating time to think, process, and produce is required. Consider attending or setting up a 'Shut up and Write' session. This is where meetups are arranged that provide designated time to write and provide social contact. They are usually facilitated through a process of dedicated writing time with breaks allocated in short periods of time to assist in productivity. Writing retreats are also another option, where dedicated time over a number of days is put aside to focus only on writing, and where daily personal and professional responsibilities are put to the side for this moment in time to assist in focus and completing writing goals. They also provide social support on many levels, including conversations about career, writing itself, feedback, etc. And another alternative is an online writing group facilitated through social media (for example, #AcWriMo or #PhDchat) where like-minded people can write with a moderation of time occurring online and writing occurring in real time with participants located anywhere. This is a great accountability process.

Communication issues

Sometimes you can feel as if your writing partner is missing in action. They may be missing a deadline, not accessible, or their communication is lacking. These situations can impede the momentum of co-writing. Good relationships take time to develop and maintain. Making time to genuinely connect and develop trust is key when working with others, and is highlighted when writing collaboratively. No matter the specific problem in why the writing may have stopped or you are feeling isolated, for example, making time for each other is vital. This is where the work of Jane Dutton (Dutton et al., 2010) and her research in high-quality connections can support the refocusing on the relationship to then approach the specific issue at hand. As we have mentioned, developing trust and a mutual respect is key to support timelines, roles and approach to collaboration. However, it is also critical to understand the psychological needs we all have to be heard, respected, and valued. We might know our own needs, but do we know the needs of our partner(s)? Dutton talks about creating micro-moments of high-quality connections to build rapport and a language you can commonly engage in when working with others (Dutton, 2003). This involves considering five key elements:

1. **Conveying presence** – being present and aware (you could engage with the strengths of awareness, humility, and curiosity).
2. **Being genuine** – to engage honestly and respectfully but being authentic to yourself (you could engage with the strengths of gratitude, honesty, perspective, and self-regulation).
3. **Communicating affirmation** - look for the positive and acknowledge this publicly (you could engage with the strengths of gratitude, kindness, and social intelligence).
4. **Effective listening** – listening with empathy, learning from other perspectives, and being active, that is, being responsive with your body language and also your words and actions (you could engage with the strengths of love of learning, perspective, zest, and bravery).
5. **Supportive communication** – requires us to be aware of what we say and how we say it while

minimising defensiveness and maximising clarity (you could engage with the strengths of judgement, fairness, forgiveness, leadership, and self-regulation).

Take it away

Collaborative writing can result in individual or collective outcomes. When partners collaborate with their own projects in mind, they look to collaborative partners for support, encouragement, and honest but friendly reviews. When partners collaborate in order to generate one outcome that reflects all of their contributions, negotiations are needed at each stage in order to integrate multiple outputs. In either situation, clearly *dialogue* is the most critical factor in collaborative writing. Writing is a very sensitive area for many people, so being able to give and receive constructive reviews of other's work is essential. Self-awareness of our own strengths and shortcomings means we can be realistic about what we commit to in the project. Reflective writing allows a place for self-monitoring and for making sense of the project as a whole. By using the Taxonomy of Collaboration as a planning tool, we can create and share maps to illustrate stages of the project.

Try it! Exercises and questions for discussion or reflection

Reflective questions and exercise

- Are you interested in working in multi-, cross-, inter- or transdisciplinary collaborative writing? Why?

- Think about a collaborative writing project you participated in as a class exercise or professional effort.
  - Define the project using terminology you have learned from this and previous chapters.
  - Use the Taxonomy to map the project.
  - What worked, what didn't? Why? What would you add or change?

References

Dutton, J. E. (2003). Fostering high-quality connections: How to deal with corrosive relationships at work. Retrieved from https://ssir.org/articles/entry/fostering_high_quality_connections.

Dutton, J. E., Roberts, L. M., & Bednar, J. (2010). Pathways for positive identity construction at work: Four types of positive identity and the building of social resources. *Academy of Management Review*, *35*(2), 265–293.

Kamler, B., & Thomson, P. (2014). *Helping doctoral students write: Pedagogies for supervision* (2nd ed.). London: Routledge.

Salmons, J. (2019). *Learning to collaborate, collaborating to learn: Engaging students in the classroom and online*. Sterling: Stylus.

8 Collaboration in the real world
Working through dilemmas of conflict, and inertia

Often when we come to the conclusion of a book, we share a summary that connects to key themes. But we have approached this last chapter in a different way. We have instead decided to engage with hypothetical dilemmas from each of our case studies (Jesse, Alicia, Elizabeth and Phillipe). As authors, we've responded to their dilemmas in a conversational manner. In doing so, we have connected with many of the ideas that explored throughout the book. We have integrated and demonstrated how the Taxonomy of Collaboration looks in action as a way to analyse the collaborative process.

As we responded to the dilemmas, we have shared some suggestions. These can also be enhanced with other suggestions we have made throughout the book. We hope that our suggestions will spark your curiosity about how you may solve similar dilemmas and conflicts. And by doing this, we acknowledge and place upfront that although we are empowering you to form, maintain, and manage productive collaborations, there will still be times when they may go pear-shaped. But you have tools to help you with this now, and hopefully a community, who can help you decode problematic situations.

168 *Collaboration in the real world*

In this chapter you will gain an understanding of:

- How to consider problem-solving collaborative dilemmas.
- Developing your toolbox of resources.
- Putting into practice learning from Chapters 1–7.
- Feeling empowered to know there is always a solution to a collaborative dilemma.

Dilemmas and problem-solving

Missing in action

Q. How can I successfully complete a collaborative project when the leader is missing in action? As part of my postdoc I am expected to work with three members of the research team. However, one of the senior researchers has been missing from the project. They don't attend meetings or answer my emails. I really want to connect with them, both for the project outcomes and also as I feel I need a relationship with them since I think they could help when it is time to look for a permanent position. – Alicia

Our responses

A. For Janet, the phenomenon of 'celebrity' academic is a familiar one. Certainly, there are top-level research leads whose main contributions are their connections and clout with funders. They don't expect to get their hands dirty with the actual work! Like it or not, others accept that the celebrity is not going to attend meetings.

Alternatively, the missing researcher might simply be neglecting the project. They are, then, neglecting the other researchers on the team. Are they concerned about the missing researcher? If they are concerned, do they plan to speak with them or take some other action? Or do they accept this behaviour because they have worked with them before, know their style, and are willing to put up with it for their own reasons?

I suggest that Alicia speak with the active senior researchers about her worries. In particular, she should discuss her needs around future employment. Are either of the other senior researchers capable of stepping in to provide the coaching and career help she needs? If they are not, where else can she turn within the institution? Perhaps another researcher would take her under their wing.

If she still wants to connect with them, I suggest trying a different communication tactic. Can Alicia request a one-to-one meeting (going through their assistant if necessary) to discuss her hopes for this research in the context of her career development?

Finally, as an early stage researcher, all experiences are learning experiences. Sometimes we learn through positive role models who inspire us to emulate their excellent work and attitudes towards others. Other times we learn from negative experiences. Janet had a profound missing-in-action experience with a dissertation supervisor. Based on that experience, she became a hands-on, supportive supervisor when she found herself in that role.

For Narelle, this case rings a couple of warning bells beyond missing communications. Firstly, it seems like there is an abuse of a power relationship here. If a senior researcher is on a project and there is an agreement that they are a part of the project, it concerns me that they are missing in action. Secondly, I am also concerned that there is a reliance on this person and reference to their career. These are two classic cases that emerge in academic where abuse of power can exist.

I would encourage Alicia to find out more as well. I would coach her to ask some key questions.

Questions for the research project:

- What is the agreed involvement of this senior researcher on the project by the team members and by the individual themself?
- What does this look like in practice for the senior researcher? How does this impact the research team?
- What are some strategies that work for the senior researcher and how could these be implemented within the research team?
- What are some negotiations that need to take place for this to work (and how can this come from all sides)?

Questions related to career development:

In terms of the need to have a relationship with this senior researcher for future employment, I encourage Alicia to consider two main things:

- **Are they the only senior researcher in your field?** Is this a researcher you want to be attached to in regard to the field AND in terms of how they behave as a researcher/academic? I say field AND behaviour as both are important here and have a part in this decision. I'm thinking *Circle of Niceness* in my response here.

- **Is this a senior researcher you will allow to treat you badly for your entire career?** Is that something you want or are willing to accept? Is there a way you can disrupt this pattern of working? And this disruption may be that you do not accept this way of working and can be empowered by working with others in the field (presuming that the original pattern of missing in action, is a common pattern and one of academic abuse).

Super-achievers

Q. How can I successfully complete a collaborative project when one partner takes over and won't let others contribute? I realise that I am only a part-time faculty member, but I am very interested in learning how to be an active contributor to collaborative projects underway in the department. However, a couple of full-time faculty members dominate meetings and don't include me when they allocate action items. How can I convince them that I am willing to work, and that they can trust me to fulfil work I commit to do? – Phillipe

Our responses

A. Narelle thinks about the situation Phillipe is in from a strengths-based perspective and connects with much of the strategies we discussed in Chapters 2 and 4. I want to encourage Phillipe to take the conversation to another level in a different context. So, if the strength of curiosity was engaged, what would be other ways Phillippe could let his colleagues know he is willing and ready to become involved in collaborative projects occurring within the department?

Utilising strengths such as zest or love of learning, Narelle would, for example, encourage Phillipe to make an appointment with the leader of a project and share his interest in contributing, indicating if this is the correct time (depending on how the project is progressing with deadlines) and offering some possibilities in what this could look like (offering both skills and strengths for the team in partnership with contribution is specific areas, for example, methodology, literature, research background, etc.).

Narelle encourages Phillipe to make connections outside of the larger meeting context. This might also be a great conversation to have with the leader of the group, especially phrased from a learning opportunity in how to work effectively with others demonstrate different approaches within a bigger context.

Janet echoes Narelle's approach, and adds another potential angle for understanding the situation. Many part-time or casual faculty members teach at multiple institutions, and are only willing to do work they are paid to complete. If they are paid to teach, they teach. They are both unwilling and unable to do more. The full-time faculty member might be taking over the project to protect Phillipe from being taken advantage of in doing unpaid work. If this is the case, he might succeed by communicating his interest in learning from experience to prepare for the next career step, as Narelle has suggested.

Team conflict

Q. How can I successfully complete a collaborative project when two partners are at odds, and can't agree on anything? – Jesse

Our responses

A. Janet sees that a conflict between two partners spills over to influence the project as a whole. She suggests that Jesse try to find out the back story on this project group, starting with how it was formed. Did these two people *choose* to be in the project, or were they assigned to it? Do they have a history of problems? If so, the conflict might have deeper roots and more complicated branches than Jesse can address.

As a junior person on the project, without the authority to direct the conflicting partners to resolve their problems, Jesse can still make suggestions that could help. For example, create a meeting format with an agenda and facilitator. Jesse can suggest voting or other types of decision-making that help to minimise openings that can devolve into conflict. Using the Taxonomy as a guide, it is possible that working in parallel would allow partners to complete parts of the project more independently.

There are some situations where other people's behaviours are beyond our control. Jesse may simply need to take steps as needed to avoid being drawn into the conflict. They can do their best to complete their part of the project, and demonstrate positive attitudes.

Narelle thinks about this situation from the perspective of active listening. What is being said (both verbally and non-verbally)? Narelle suggests connecting with the strategies when from Chapter 4 associated with active listening. Compassion and holding the space to listen with their heart, head, and ears will allow Jesse to be open and focus on what is being said. Narelle thinks that at times like this, when we know there is some tension in the room, it is important to be aware of what is perhaps sensitivity to conflict, the delivery style of the other person, or a disagreement about strategy.

Setting a communication protocol based on taking turns is important and key. Listen with curiosity. Repeat back, 'so what I hear you say it … and repeat the key aspects'. Confirm back and forth. Often in this process there can be some negotiations that occur as there will naturally be some language changes and the need to clarify. Then as you continue to repeat this process a few times, take the time to then share your perspective. This takes time.

You have to invest in doing this. Negotiation takes time. It is worthy of your attention to take the time. And while holding the space, you can both find a solution, which may be to agree to respectfully disagree. Use these negotiations to learn from and with each other – sharing your strengths, how you see the world, how you can problem solve, how you prefer to work together, etc. Communication is key.

Narelle also acknowledges that sometimes we need to mindfully step away, and say 'I need some time to process' or 'I would like to talk about this at another time' and then come back to it.

Commitment obstacles

Q. How can I successfully complete a collaborative project when a person critical to the project won't commit to the agreement? They think we should just get on with the project, and don't see the need to plan or make agreements. – Elizabeth

Our responses

A. In the situation Elizabeth finds herself in, Janet suggests that the first question is 'Why?' Is the hold-off based on the timelines, roles, or other parts of the agreement? Or is it an objection to planning, period? In the first instance, the problematic sections can be discussed and, if necessary, revised.

If the planning process is the obstacle, step back and reflect on options for moving forward.

Janet observes that there are groups who can work organically, without an explicit plan. Collaborative partners have worked together, or have already established trust and respect. They operate in a field where there are widely accepted practices which would be known to all partners. Has Elizabeth come into such an established group? If so, she could ask partners to tell about what they've done previously, and how it went. By listening and asking questions, she can learn their implicit code for working collaboratively.

On the other hand, it is possible that this person's working style is action-oriented, and they find planning to be a waste of time. It is true that some groups can have seemingly endless discussions to wordsmith perfect mission and purpose statements, taking time away from the project itself. Is there a way to compromise?

Are there parts of the agreement Elizabeth feels are essential for her to trust that the process for completing the collaborative project will be fair and respectful? Can she negotiate with the recalcitrant partner to sign off on those specific parts of the agreement? Alternatively, can she negotiate a sequential approach with process and project checkpoints? If all is well at these checkpoints, they continue; if problems are identified, they agree to define and address them before proceeding.

Narelle agrees with Janet and offers the perspective that this type of collaboration situation is one that is worthy of attention to finding out the *why* this is occurring. I want to ask: Has the work been done on the skills and strengths that each person brings to the collaboration? Has time been made for these discussions? Can time be made to have this discussion now if it hasn't, or could time be now made to reconnect to the discussion that did occur to reconnect and tweak ways to move forward? Conversation and deep listening are key here as progressing with the collaboration for both outcomes and the experience is crucial for satisfaction for Elizabeth, and ideally the collaborator(s). It may be a tricky conversation, but can be undertaken in a way that embraces a mutual respect to learn from one another in how to best move forward.

What other approaches would you suggest for working through these dilemmas? What strengths and skills will you draw on to become the partner everyone will want on their projects?

Take it away

You might encounter dilemmas such as these, or others we haven't described. We hope our suggestions help you and spark possibility while also acknowledging these are a starting point, and that there are indeed many ways you can approach collaborative dilemmas. As you consider how you navigate your collaborations, we have some tips to guide you:

- Don't think the worst.
- Be careful not to create stories (you know when your mind chatter heads into 'What if?' scenarios and periods of rumination).

- Seek advice.
- Find a way to talk to the person and tell them how you feel 'I messages'.
- Stop and step back (awareness is key, and remember that you don't have to respond on the spot).
- Build your toolbox of resources to approach dilemmas associated to collaborations.
- There is always more than one way to view a situation so it's always worth looking at other perspectives.
- Don't sit on a dilemma and let it get out of control.
- Don't blame or finger point; remember mutual respect and that you are always learning from a situation, even if it is not ideal.
- You have the power in determining how you react.
- Be aware of your strengths, and how you can learn from others who have different strengths to you or utilise the same strengths as you in different ways.
- Have an awareness of your skills and those of others.
- What are your values and how will this then transfer to your collaborations?
- What's your routine, and how does this support or hinder your collaborations?
- If you have to, and you can, it is OK to walk away. What are your boundaries in terms of what you are going to accept in how you are treated?
- And always think: What good behaviours or *Circle of Niceness* are you going to model and pass on to others?

Parting words

In this book we have invited you to pause and mindfully reflect upon how you approach collaborations. We have

Collaboration in the real world 179

invited you to rethink and reframe collaboration. We have challenged you with new ideas and drawn on a Taxonomy of Collaboration and strengths-based research to support your approach to collaboration. It is our hope you feel more confident when you go into situations of collaboratively working with people you either know or don't know. We hope this will show you that you can grow as part of the collaborative process when you navigate project development and outcomes while also embracing planning for approach. We know dilemmas will emerge, and we hope that you see these as learning opportunities, not as blockers that stop you from enjoying fruitful possibilities.

Appendix 1

> **Case study connection: Working collaboratively and building skills and strengths**

This table provides you with some reflective questions to support your approach to collaboration across a number of different areas. They provide you with a starting point to consider how you can approach collaboration, and can be transferred across contexts and also expanded on as you work with these ideas.

		Co-writing or editing	Co-research	Postdoc	Professional or department team
Low trust	Mindful reflection	What strengths do I have that I can utilise for co-writing? What strengths of the team members support my strengths? What can I learn from others?	What possibilities exist for me to bring my strengths to a co-research opportunity?	How can I find out the strengths that my team has? What work may have been done before to identify these? What do I notice in how the team works?	What energises and excites me about working with this team? What skills do I have that may be an asset to the team that will support approaching the task at hand?
	Dialogue	How can I use the strength of communication in working with a partner(s) to plan the writing?	What strengths do my co-researchers have? What can I notice in how they engage or speak? What explicit conversations can we have to highlight co-researchers' strengths?	How might I approach becoming a part of the team and highlighting strengths that energise us? As I am working with the team, what conversations can we have that centre around our strengths and what we bring to the team?	What might be possible when we talk about strengths that allow us to showcase positivity and energy in how we approach the task at hand?

(Continued)

	Co-writing or editing	Co-research	Postdoc	Professional or department team
Review	How can I establish a process that builds constructive mutual critique and incorporate others' perspectives in the co-writing process? What protocols will I need to agree upon for successfully acknowledging your strengths?	As you and your co-researchers work together and begin to produce work, what will the process be to support constructive feedback? What will success look like for the collaboration?	As a team how will I contribute to the consideration of which elements of each partner's work should be included in the final deliverables, and how the pieces will be integrated into the final work? What skills and strengths come into play for me and my team members?	How will your team approach provide feedback to each of your team members contributions? What skills and strengths come into play for you and your team members?

(Continued)

	Co-writing or editing	Co-research	Postdoc	Professional or department team
Parallel collaboration	As you work on your co-writing project, have you allocated sections of the project that showcase all collaborators' strengths? How might this approach support a combined effort? What will success look like?	As you work on your research project, what strengths and skills can you utilise to support your own momentum and that of the collaborators when dividing the project into parts that can be completed separately? How will I approach joining these parts back together for flow of communication style? What will success look like?	How can I support the team to build on skills and strengths that energise everyone when dividing up tasks? What will success look like?	As you work on different sections of the task, what protocols need to be put into place to support the elements that are combined into a collective final product? Is there an approach you can make that utilises partners strengths and skill sets to support momentum and meeting of deadlines? What will success look like?

(Continued)

	Co-writing or editing	Co-research	Postdoc	Professional or department team
Sequential collaboration	As you work on your co-writing project, you work with you partners to divide the work into parts that can be completed in stages over a defined time frame. What strengths are highlighted in working this way for you and your collaborators? What strengths come into fruition as you navigate building on each other's contributions through a series of progressive steps? What might this look like?	As you work on your research collaboration, there will be times when you need to come back together to check in and make sure everyone is on the same vision, what strengths come into play that you have identified in the team to ascertain success? What negotiations may need to occur?	As you move through a task, there will be moments where a meeting needs to be held to address how all parts of the project are combined into a collective final product or the process moves to another level of collaboration, how will a strengths-based approach come into play? What do you and the team members need to be aware of in moving from individual to sequential collaboration?	How can you and the team divide the work into parts that can be completed in stages over a defined time frame? What protocols need to be put in place to support momentum, deadlines being met and consistency?

(Continued)

	Co-writing or editing	Co-research	Postdoc	Professional or department team
High trust	Synergistic collaboration	As you work on your co-writing/co-research/pos-doc/or professional team project, you will work with your partners to synthesise their ideas to plan, organise and complete the creation of a product that melds all contributions into a collective final product. How will I approach the utilising of strengths of each member of the collaboration? What will success look like? What ways of working may I have to put in place to support this way of working? How can I engage with establishing and maintaining trust? What might this look like for your collaboration?		

Index

Page numbers in **bold** refer to content in **tables**. Page numbers in *italics* refer to content in *figures*.

academic collaboration 32–34
accountability 5, 80, 111, 163
autonomy 42–45
awareness 54, 78, *89*, 164; see also self-awareness

best practice 100, 120, 143, 160, *161*
blogs xxv, 65, 88
Bloom's Taxonomy (1956/2000) 107–108, **108**, 111–112, 115–116
boundaries 43; working across 1, 4, 5–7, *7*, 8, 19, 38, 114, 132, 145, *146*, 149
burnout 26–27

calendars 133, 135–136, 139, 140
capability (postgraduate study) **65**
career development 168, 169, 170–171
case studies: Alicia (postdoc) 15, **17**, 20, 66–67, 92–93, 112–113, 114, 140, 154–155, 167, 168–171; Elizabeth (early career researcher) 16, **17**, 20, 35, 90–91, 113–114, 141, 155, 167, 175–177; Jesse (early career researcher) 16, **17**, 20, 35–36, 92, 113, 114, 141, 167, 173–175; Philippe (PhD student/contract university teacher) 15, **17**, 20, 66–67, 91, 112, 114, 139–140, 167, 171–173
case study connection 180, **181**–**185**
celebrity academic 168–169; see also faculty hierarchy
Cheek, J. 142
choice 42, 43, 89
Circle of Niceness xx, 63, 64, 75, 100, 171, 178; mapped *89*; spreading good academic behaviour 88–90
collaboration xiv–xxiii; boundaries (within and across) 5–7; big picture 24–26; characterisation 2–3; core issues xxii–xxiii; definition (Gray) 2; definition (Salmons) 3,

11, 105, 150; fundamentals 1–22; 'going beyond' xv; mixed results xvii; nature and dynamics xiv–xv; overcoming negative assumptions xvi; reframed in positive way xiv, xix, xxii; strengths-based 23–50; versus 'group effort' xv–xvi; workings 3–5
collaboration: importance 17–19; addressing social problems 19; research and writing 17–18; teaching 18–19
collaboration dynamics 45
collaborative advantage 7, 41, 126; factors supporting **9–10**; meta, meso, or micro levels 8–11
collaborative e-learning 106
collaborative inertia 7–8, 20, 26, 41, 77, 126, 134, 138, 149; factors enabling **9–10**; meta, meso, or micro levels 8–11; strategies to overcome 142–144
Collaborative Knowledge Learning Model 127, 128
collaborative knowledge learning in research context *127*
collaborative learning (and teaching) 104–123; big picture 105–107; current thinking 114–115; definition (Salmons) 105; exercises 120–122; gaining skills 116–117; off- and online 115; pitfalls 119–120; practice 114–120; using conceptual models for instruction **117–118**
collaborative learning: theories and models 107–112; Bloom's taxonomy 107–108; Salmons (2019) 108–110; Taxonomy of Collaboration 110–112
collaborative learning experiences: design 107–112
collaborative research 20, 124–147; big picture 125–126; building skills and strengths **181–185**; cases and examples 139–141; exercises 145–146; nature 127–129; pitfalls 144–145; practice 142–144
collaborative research across disciplines 129–133; levels of disciplinarity 130–133
collaborative research tools 133–139; files, folders, and calendars 135; systems, software, and access 134–135; technology 138–139; version control 135–136; wikis 136–138, 139
collaborative research transition 124

collaborative work: as new faculty member 20; as postdoc or intern 20
collaborative writing 20, 148–166; big picture 149–150; building skills and strengths **181**–**185**; cases and examples 154–155; exercises 165–166; individual and collective outcomes 152–154; leadership and decision-making 150–152; obstacles 149; practice 156–160
collaborative writing: pitfalls 162–165; communication issues 163–165; feelings of isolation 162; hard to find time 163; idea flow issues 162
collaborative writing: work plans 157–160; parallel approach *157*, 157–158; sequential approach *158*, 158–159; synergistic approach 159, *159*
collegiality 36, 88, *89*, 90, 124, 144
commitment obstacles 175–177
communication **9**, 13, 41, 45, **61**, **65**, 78, 156–157, 163–165, 169, 175, **181**; with free riders 96–97; individual responsibility 38, 40; postgraduate study **65**; *see also* information and communication technologies

communication problems 97–99, 149
communication response matrix **98**
communication styles xiv, 40, 97
complexity xv, 4–5, 6, 14, 35, 64, 81, 125, 126, 133, 144, 150, 160
conceptual knowledge 107, **108**, **117**
conflict-resolution 44–45, 47, 76, 97, 133, 173–175
consistency (postgraduate study) **65**
conversation 67, 68, 79, 80, **82**, 91, 94, 144, 163, 172, 177, **181**
creativity xix, 32–33; mind map **33**
credibility 119–120
cross-disciplinarity *130*, 131, 132, 146
culture **9**, 11
curiosity xix, 25, **28**, 34, 41, 54, 78, 92, 164, 172
curriculum development 18–19, 20

deadlines xx, 34, 66, 77–78, 149, 156, 163, 172; *see also* time
Deci, E. L. 45
decision-making 150–152
deficit-based approach 25–26
dialogue *xviii*, 11, *12*, 13, *111*, **117**–**118**, 165, **181**; collaborative writing (best practice) *161*; thinking about strengths *39*

discipline (field of study) xiv, xxi, 6, 8, **9**, 19, 60, **61**, 62, **108**, 114, 121, 133, 142, 145, 162; *see also* multidisciplinarity

doctoral students xiv, xx, xxi, 1, 24, 31, 81, 94, 104, 124, 160; approaches to relationship support **61**; career aspirations 56–59; collaborating across 63–65, 67, 70, 72; collaborating up 60–63, 70, 71–72; collaboration expectation 81; exercises 71–72; impact 57; PhD experience 51–74; practice 68–70; purpose 56–59; satisfaction 56–59; social media support groups 64, **65**; Three Cs of postgraduate study 64, **65**

drafts 4, 77–78, 122, 137, 151, 154, 159; *see also* version control

Dropbox 135

Dutton, J. E. 164

e-learning 106

early career researchers xiv, xix, xxi, 19, 20, 24, 31, 34, 60, 62–63, 94, 114, 124, 126, 160, 162; collaboration expectation 81; collaborative teaching and learning 104; *see also* case-studies

emotion **61**, 68

empathy 77, **82**, 99, 164

empowerment xvi, xix, 59, 81, 167, 171

energisation 24, 25, 31, **32**, 33, 35, 37, 69, 70, 79, 80, 90, **181**

energy levels 26, 43

enjoyment 2, 20, 23, 25, 33, 57, *89*, 142

exchange 3, **9**; *see also* knowledge exchange

exercises: collaboration in academic life 21; collaboration skills and strengths 46–47; collaborative research 145–146; collaborative teaching and learning 120–122; collaborative writing 165–166; doctoral students 71–72; working as group 99–100

Facebook 64

factual knowledge 107, **108**, **117**

faculty hierarchy xiv, 119–120; *see also* power relationships

failure: use as motivation 80

feedback 4, 162, **182**

Five Ways to Wellbeing (NEF, 2010) 53–54, **54**

forming a 'we' *xviii*, xix, xxi

free riders 96–97

Fromm, E. 98

full-timers 16, **17**, 171, 173

generosity 4, 109, 155

gratitude xix, 25, 34, 35, 79, 88, *89*, 164

Gray, B. 2

habit 55, 80

Hafernik, J. J. 142

Hanganu-Opatz, I. L. 143
health 86; *see also* PERMAH
Hibbert, P. 44
high stakes xix, 5, 143, 156
higher education xvi, xvii, xx, xxv, 1, 23, 24, 25, 31, 38, 43, 53, 57, 59, 60, 78, 80, 81, 88, 89, 104
Hoffman, D. 138
honesty xix, 25, 90, 164; 'strength' versus 'skill' 76–77
hope (strength) **28**, 81, **82**, 90–91
humility xix, 25, **28**, **83**, 92, 164
humour **28**, 35, 36, **82**
Huxham, C. 7–8, 44, 143

identity 85–86
Ikigai (reason for being) 69
imposter syndrome 66
individual responsibilities 38–41
individual work within team 37–38
individualism 11
informal interactions 143–144
information and communication technologies (ICTs) 106, 115, 138; *see also* communication
instructors 104, 105, 106, 109–110, 119, 120–121
intellectual property 77
inter-group context 6, *7*
interdisciplinarity *130*, 131, 132, 146
internet 18–19, 27, 106, 114, 115, 134–135

interns 20, 114, 116
intra-group context 6, *7*
isolation 26, 34, 63, 86, 162, 164

Jarden, A. 71
Jeanes, E. 125
job crafting 57–59
job satisfaction 26–27, 85
Jose, P. E. 71
judgement **28**, 35–36, **40**, 41, 44, **84**, 165

Kabat-Zinn, J. 29
Kamler, B. 160
Kanter, R. M. 2–3
Kashdan, T. B. 71
Kern, P. 81–87
kindness **28**, 41, **82**, 88, *89*, 164
knowledge 5, 105
knowledge acquisition 109, 110, **117–118**, 127, 128
knowledge co-creation *109*, 110, **117–118**, 127, *127*, 128
knowledge dimensions 107, **108**
knowledge exchange 109, *109*, 116, **117–118**, *127*, 127–128
knowledge learning **117–118**
knowledge transfer 109, *109*, 116, **117–118**, 120, *127*, 128

laws and regulations **9**
Leadbeater, C. W. 127
leadership 6, 143, 149, 150–152

Lemon, N. 88, 170–172, 174–177; academic collaboration 32–34; background xxiv–xxv; creativity (strength) 32–33; journey as co-author xvii–xxi; strengths 25
Lingard, L. 144
listening xx, **83**, 90, 97, 98–99, 133, 164, 174, 176, 177
love of learning **28**, 35, **84**, 92, 164, 172

managing: individual responsibility 38, 40
McQuaid, P. 81–87
mentoring 59, 60, 62, 63, 70, 72, **89**, 109, 128, 143
metacognitive knowledge **108**, 108, **118**
Mewburn, I. 88
Migration, Displacement & Education (UN Global Education Monitoring, 2019) 121–122
mindful reflection *111*, **181**; thinking about strengths *39*; writing (best practice) *161*
mindfulness xxiv, 13, 41–42, 43, 54; as collective 78–79; definition 29; individual work within team 37–38; parts 29–30; practice 36–45; and strengths 29–31; supportive versus unsupportive collaborations **40**
missing in action 168–171

More Knowledgeable Other (Vygotsky) 128–129
motivation 26–27, 42, 45, 80
multidisciplinarity 18–19, *130*, 131, 143, 146

new faculty members 20, 114, 124, 143
non-governmental organisations (NGOs) 8, **9**, 16, 35, 141, 155
non-judgementalism 29, 30, 37, **40**, 78

openness **9–10**, 30, 62, 64, 70, 78, 81, 90, 99, 133, 174
organisational culture 80–87
organising: individual responsibility 38, 40
outcomes: individual versus collective 3

Palmer, S. 88
parallel collaboration *xviii*, 12, 13, *111*, 116, **117**, 175, **183**; thinking about strengths *39*; writing (best practice) *161*
parallel work design 122
part-timers 99, 171, 172
partners xv–xvi, xix, xx–xxi, xxii, 3, 4, 13–14, 18, 20, 24, 30, 34, 46, 53, 87, 133, 134–135, 165; commitment to 77–78; mindfulness tips 79–80; positive relations 44–45; selection 41–42; working as group 99–100
Pérez, J. 129, 136–137
PERMA (Seligman) 81

PERMAH (McQuaid and Kern) 56, 81–87; Positive emotions 81, **82**, 85; Engagement **82**, 85; Relationships **83**, 85–86; Meaning **84**, 86; Accomplishment **84**, 86–87; Health 81, **84**, 87
perseverance: 'strength' versus 'skill' 77
perspectives xiv, xix, 4, 25, 27, 35, 36, **40**, 43, 44, 75, 99, 107, 131, 132, 133, 142, 152, 160, 162, 164, 178
Peterson, C. 27–29
Pitt, R. 88
planning xvi, 55, 92–93, 133, 151, 156, 157–160, 175–176, 179; individual responsibility 38, 40–41
positive psychology 25, 29, 85
postdoctoral researchers 19, 20, 60, 63, 119; building skills and strengths 181–185; *see also* case studies
power relationships 62, 170; *see also* celebrity academic
practice: collaboration in academic life 17–18; collaboration skills and strengths 36–45; collaborative research 142–144; collaborative teaching 114–120; strengths and mindfulness (keys to collaborative advantage) 36–45; collaborative writing 156–160; PhD experience 68–70; working as group 93–94
problem-solving 5, 44, 45, 70–71, 72, 76, 97; commitment obstacles 175–177; missing in action 168–171; suggestions 177–178; super-achievers 171–173; team conflict 173–175
procedural knowledge 107, **108**, **118**
process (concept) 11
Proctor, R. W. 125–126, 132–133, 143
professional or department team: building skills and strengths **181–185**
Project 'let's work together' 34

reflection *xviii*, 11, 12, 13, 80; individual work within team 37–38
reflection in action 93, 94
reflective questions 21, 37, 38, **40**, 41, 69, 96, 165–166, 180
Reframing Collaboration in Higher Education and Beyond: about this book xiv–xxiii; book hopes xiv, xv, xvi, xxi, xxiii, 20; book perspective xvi; book scope xxi–xxiii; book website xxiii; way to read book xxi–xxiii
relationships 26, 34, **40**, 51, 56, 62–72 *passim*, 88, **89**, 90, 170; key to wellbeing 59–60; support and needs **61**; *see also* PERMAH

research and writing 17–18
respect 4, 11, 44, 62, 64, 68, 75, 88, *89*, 90, 98, 104, 119, 164, 176, 178
responsibilities 18, 31, 38–41, 53, 80, 126, 134, 139, 140, 158, 163
review *xviii*, 11, *12*, 13, *111*, **117**, **182**; thinking about strengths *39*; writing (best practice) *161*
rumination 67, 68, 177
Ryan, R. M. 45

Salmons, J. 168–169, 172–176; background xxv–xxvi; collaborative learning model (2019) 108–110; connecting skills and strengths 77–78; journey as co-author xvii–xxi; strengths xix, 25
Schön, D. A. 94
self-awareness xix–xx, 30–31, 41, 145, 165; *see also* awareness
self-care 51, 52–55, 57, 59, 71, 72, 126; and beyond 55–56; core 53; worthy of our attention *52*
self-care routines **54**, 55–56, 59, **61**, 67, 69–70; connecting with others 63
self-determination theory 45
self-improvement 30, 78
self-regulation 42–43, 164, 165
Seligman, M. E. P. 27–29
sequential collaboration *xviii*, *12*, 13–14, *111*, 116, **117**, **184**; thinking about strengths *39*; writing (best practice) *161*
sequential work design 122
Sheldon, K. M. 71
silos **9**, *33*, 34
skills 23–26, 31–32, 36, 38, *39*, 46, 75–76, **181–185**; 'character traits' 31; versus 'strengths' 24, **32**; wellbeing framework 81–87
skills development **61**
social intelligence 92, 164
social media xxiv, 163
software 134–135, 139, 157
Spence, G. B. 42
strength spotting 37, 79, 109
strengths 23–50, 69, 75–76, **181–185**; definition 25, 31; mindfulness tips for working with partners 79; practice 36–45; reflection using VIA character strengths tool 27–29; versus 'skills' 24, **32**; wellbeing framework 81–87
strengths-based perspective 88, 100, 172, 179
Strengths Profiler 32
super-achievers 171–173
supervisors 51, 55–56, 59, 60, 62, 64, 66, 67, 68, 70, 71–72, 91
support xiv, xvi, xx, 24, 34, 36, *89*
synergistic collaboration *xviii*, *12*, 14, *111*, 116, **117**, **185**; thinking about strengths *39*; writing (best practice) *161*

synergistic work design 122

tacit knowledge 6
Taxonomy of Collaboration (Salmons, 2019) xv–xvi, xvii, 30, 38, 93, 110–112, 116, **117–118**, 121, 148, 167, 174, 179; building skills and strengths 180, **181–185**; collaborative writing 156–160, 165, 166; collective and individual outcomes 152, *153*; elements 110, *111*; levels of collaboration *111*; processes 110, *111*; putting process and organisation together 11–14; teaching and learning *111*; thinking about strengths *39*; work design options 110, *111*
Taxonomy of Educational Objectives (Bloom et al., 1956) 107
teaching 18–19
teaching assistants 114, 116, 120–121
teaching and learning 104–123; *see also* collaborative learning
team conflict 173–175
teamwork: not precisely synonymous with 'collaboration' 105
tension **40**, 45, 57, 62, 67, 71, 142, 144, 174
Thomson, P. 160
time xix, 2, 16, 17, 23, 24, 29, 32, 42, 45, 52–58 *passim*, **65**, 81, **83**, 96, 110, 112, 114, 116, 122, 133, 138, 140, 144, 150, 153, 155, 157, 158, 174–175, 176, 177, **184**; *see also* deadlines
time management **61**, 64, 163
time zones 4, 126
timelines 5, **10**, 67, **68**, **84**, 97, 164, 175
transdisciplinarity *130*, 131, 132, 146
trust *xviii*, xx, 4–5, **10**, *12*, 14, *39*, 44–45, 78, *89*, *111*, 116, 121, 138, 149, 156, *161*, 163, 164, 176, **181–185**; essential to successful collaboration 105
Twitter xxiii, 64, 88

United Nations Global Education Monitoring 121–122
US National Academy of Sciences 129–130

Values-in-Action (VIA) 27–29, 32, 37; strengths list **28**
Vangen, S. 7–8
version control 135–136, 139, 157; *see also* drafts
video 137
videoconferencing 96, 106, 115
Vu, K.-P. L. 125–126, 132–133, 143
Vygotsky, L. S. 128

Walton, H. 55, 64
weakness 25, 26, 66, 145
web conferencing 134–135

wellbeing: character strengths required 71; effect of organisational culture 80–81; importance of relationships 59–60; PERMAH framework 81–87
wikis 136–138, 139; definition 136
Wood, D. 2
working collaboratively and building skills and strengths 180, **181**–**185**
working as group: aligning strengths 95; big picture 76–78; exercises 99–100; practice 93–94; skills and strengths 75–103
working as group: common problems 96–99; freeloaders 96–97; miscommunication 97–99
working together (concept) 11
workplace wellbeing 57–59

Young, S. 129, 136–137
'your why' 51, 56–59, **61**, 67, 69, 72

zest xix, 25, **28**, 35, **82**, 91, 164, 172

For Product Safety Concerns and Information please contact our EU representative GPSR@taylorandfrancis.com
Taylor & Francis Verlag GmbH, Kaufingerstraße 24, 80331 München, Germany

www.ingramcontent.com/pod-product-compliance
Lightning Source LLC
Chambersburg PA
CBHW060604230426
43670CB00011B/1964